Literary Paintings

Artworks influenced by literature

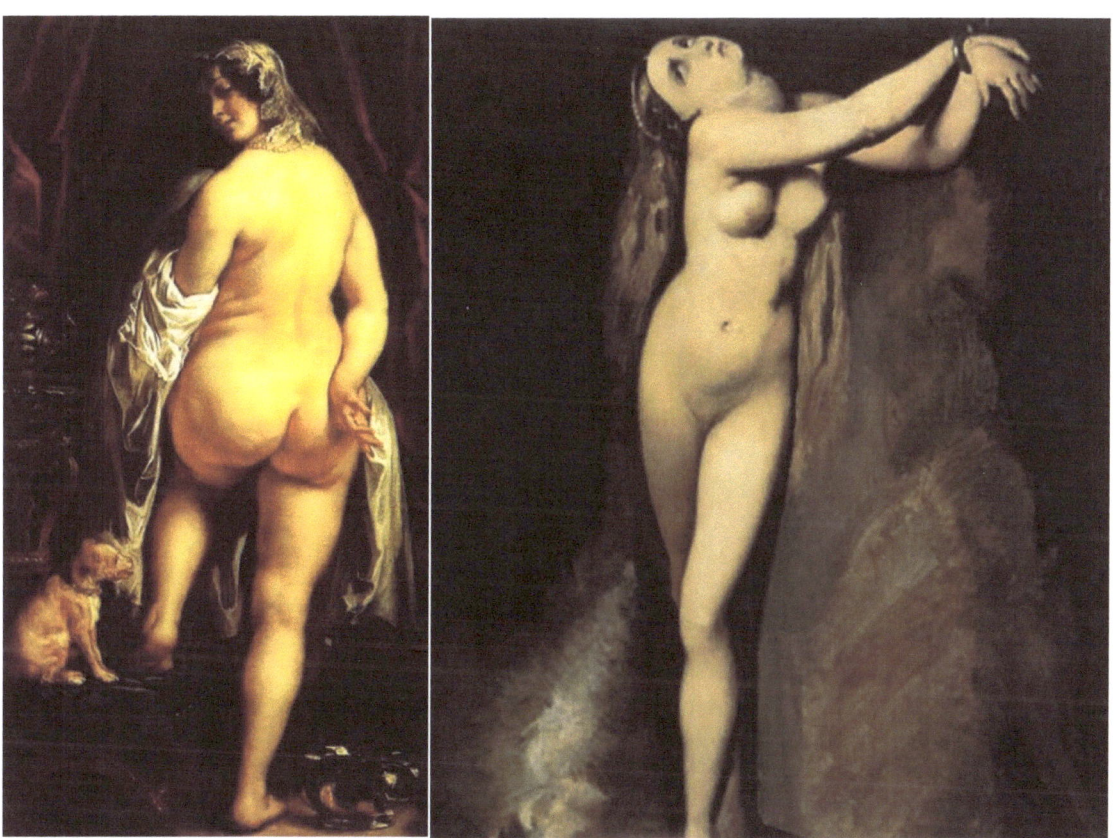

Edited by Lacey Belinda Smith

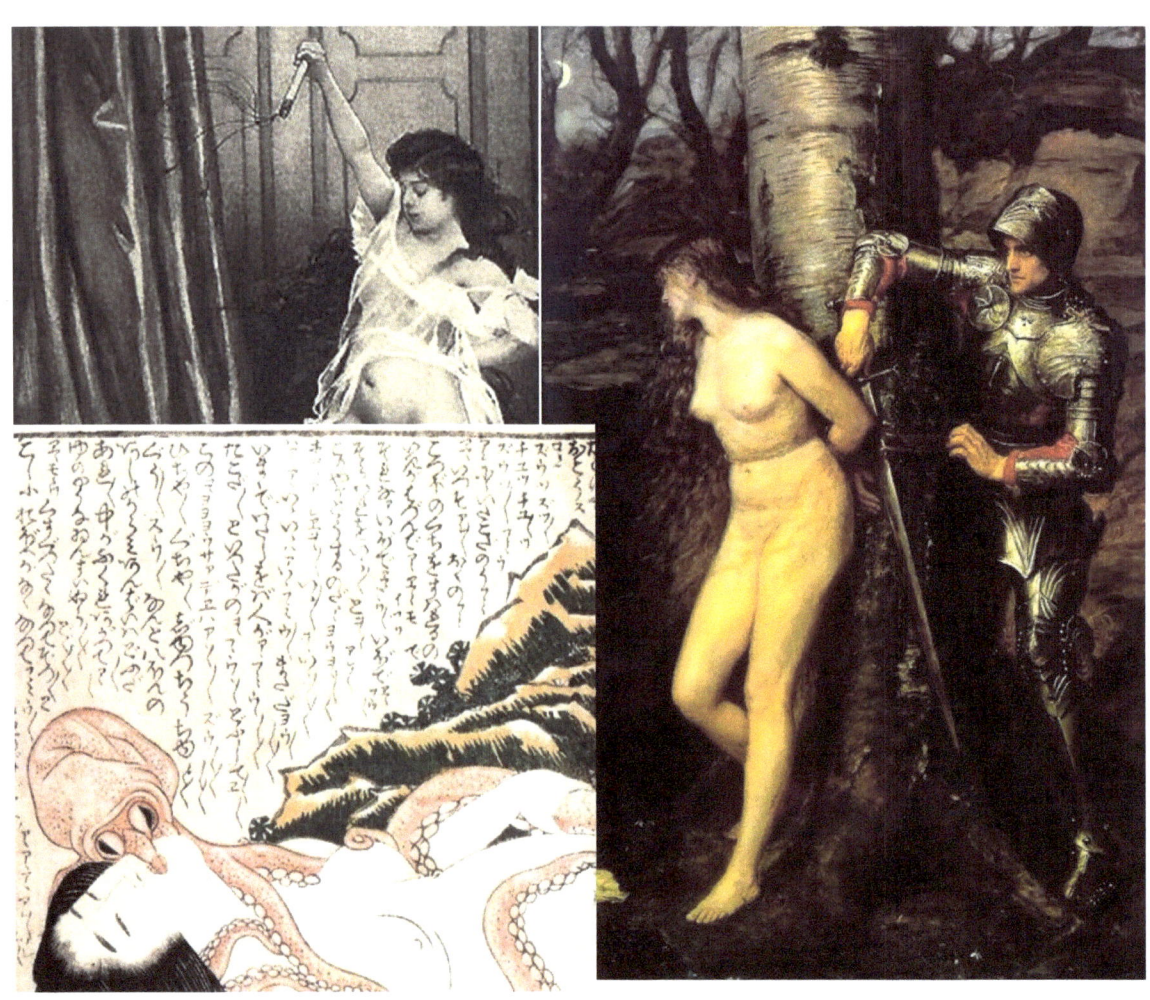

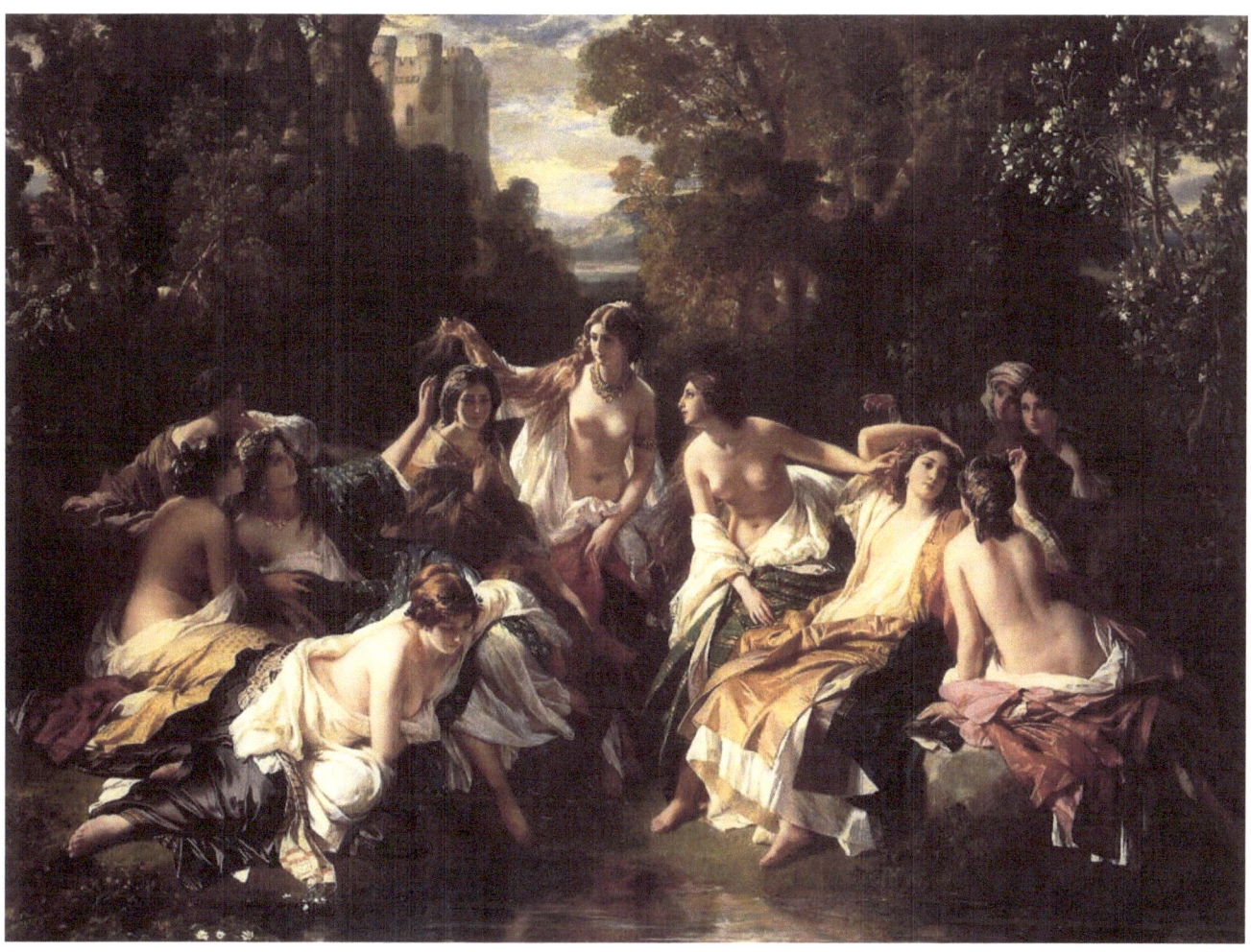

Florinda--Franz Xaver Winterhalter—1853--Neoclassicism

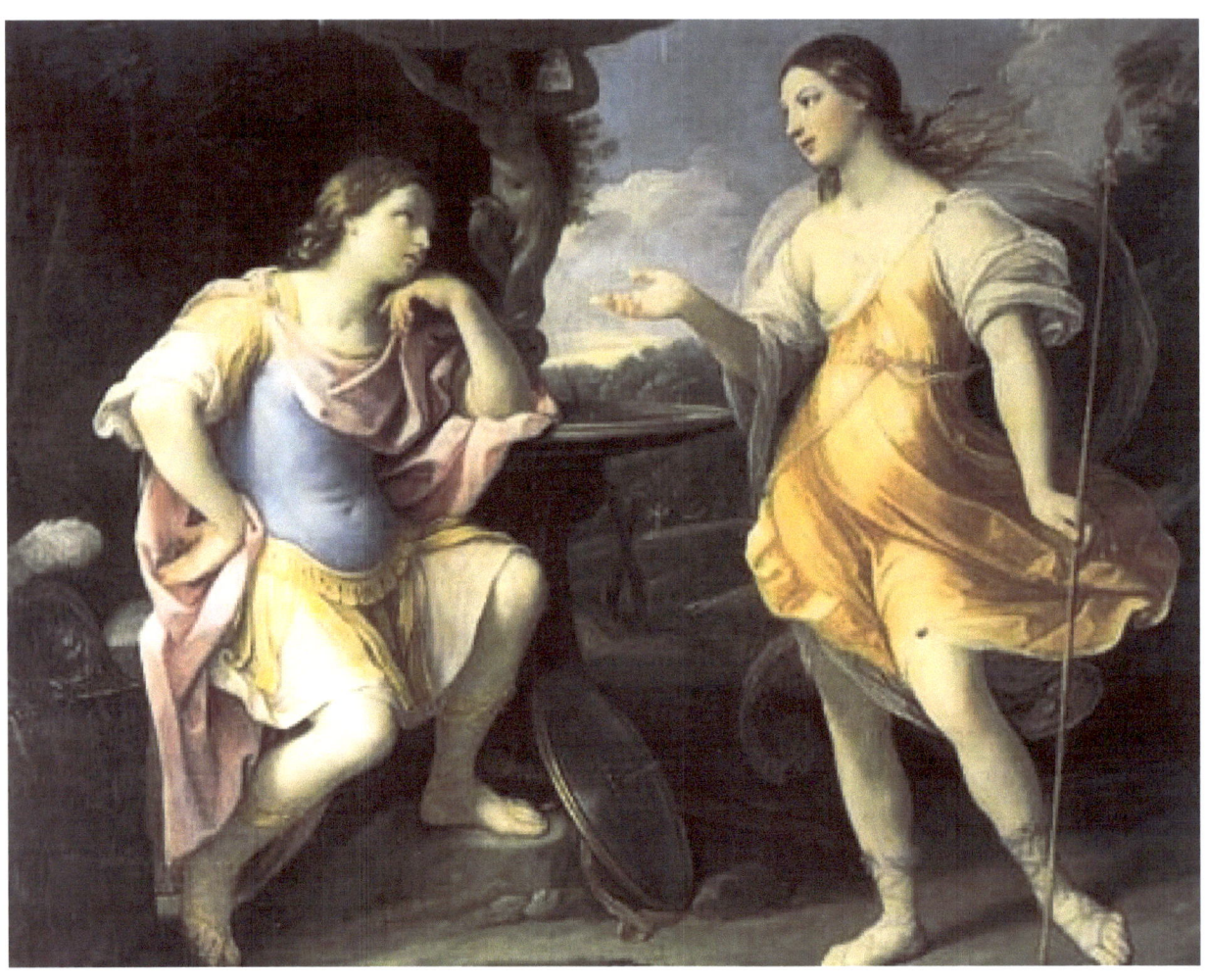

Encounter of Bradamante and Fiordispina--Guido Reni—1635--Baroque

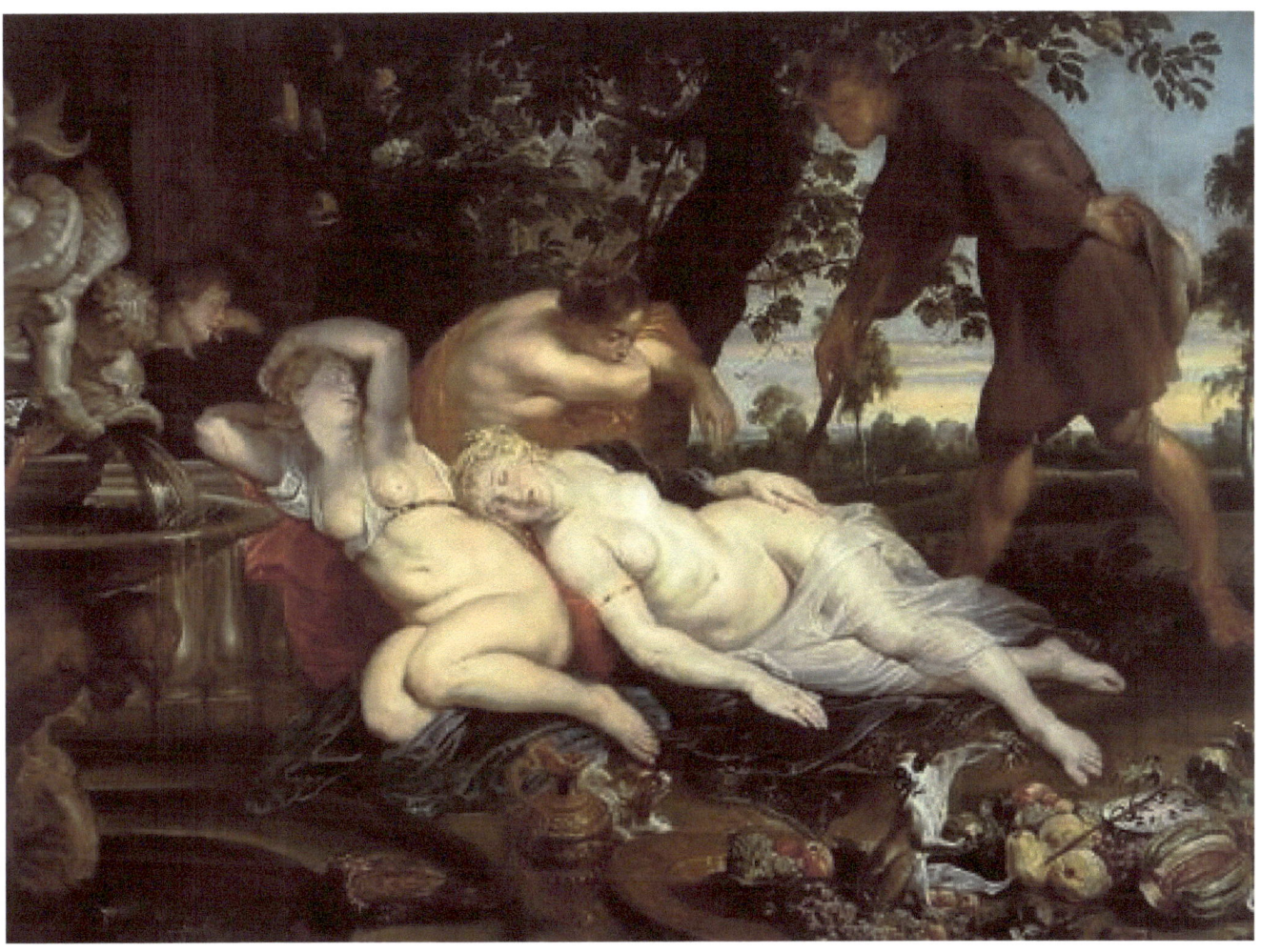

Cymon and Iphigenia--Frans Snyders-- Baroque--1617

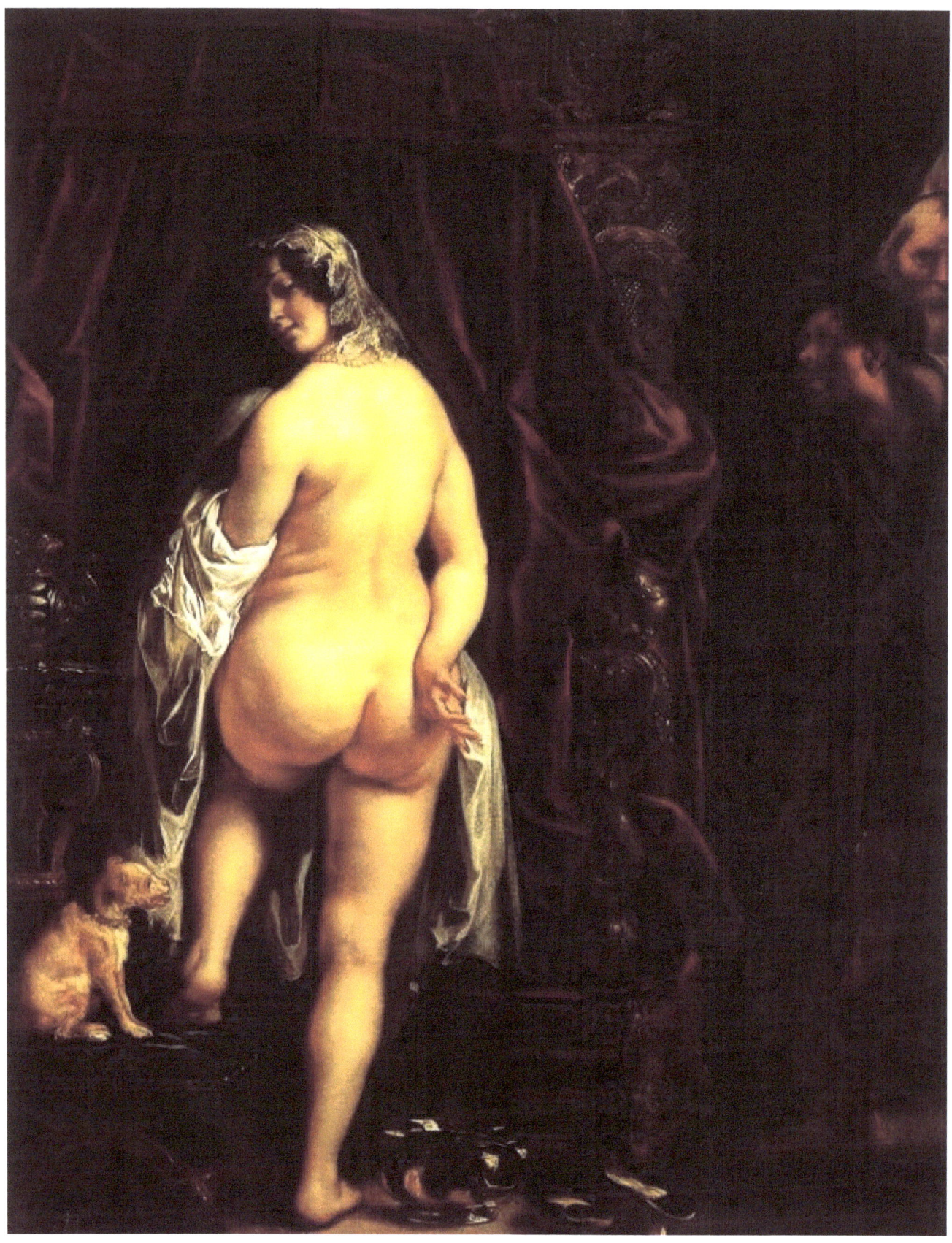

King Candaules of Lydia Showing his Wife to Gyges--Jacob Jordaens—1646--Baroque

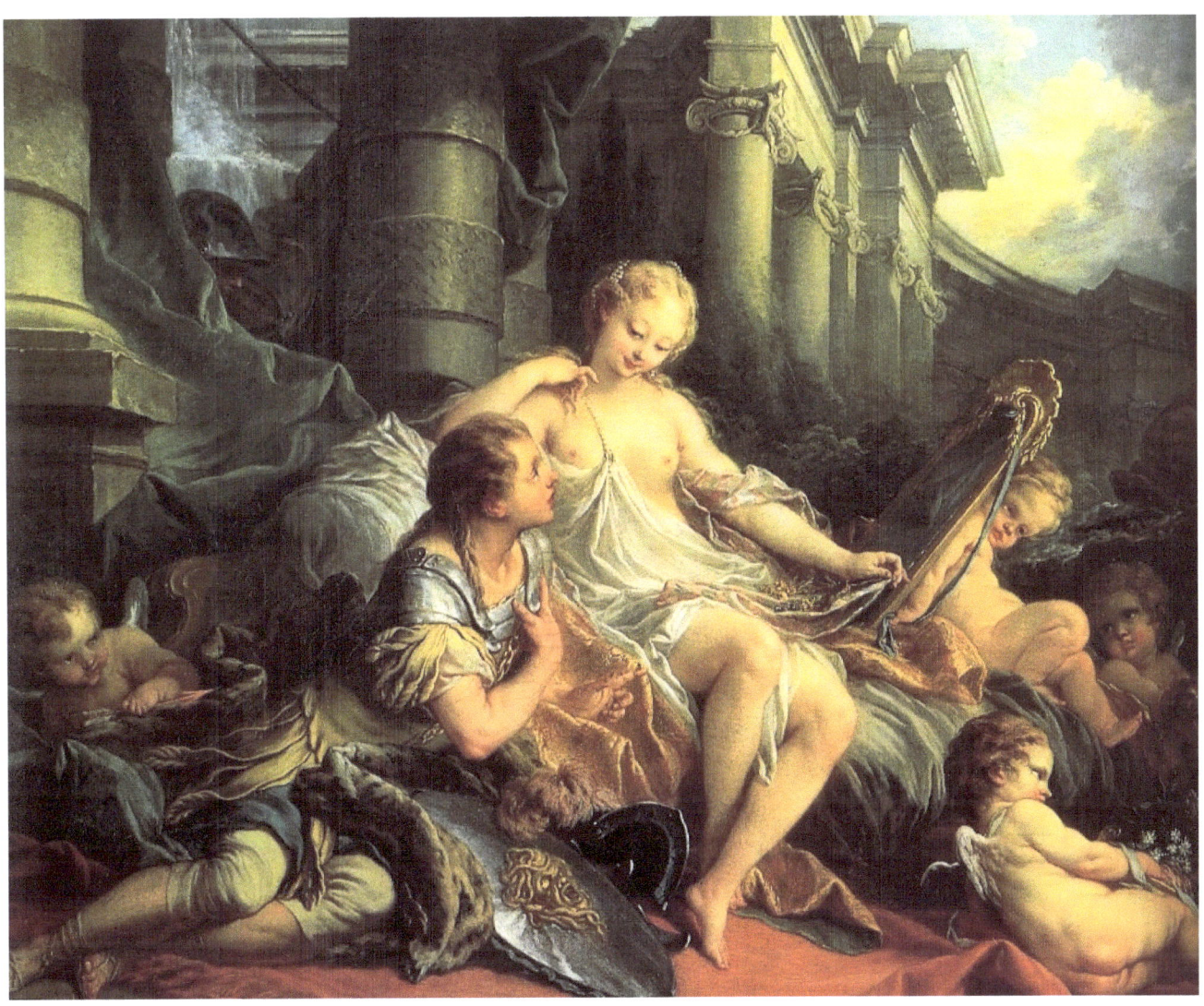

Rinaldo and Armida--Francois Boucher--Rococo

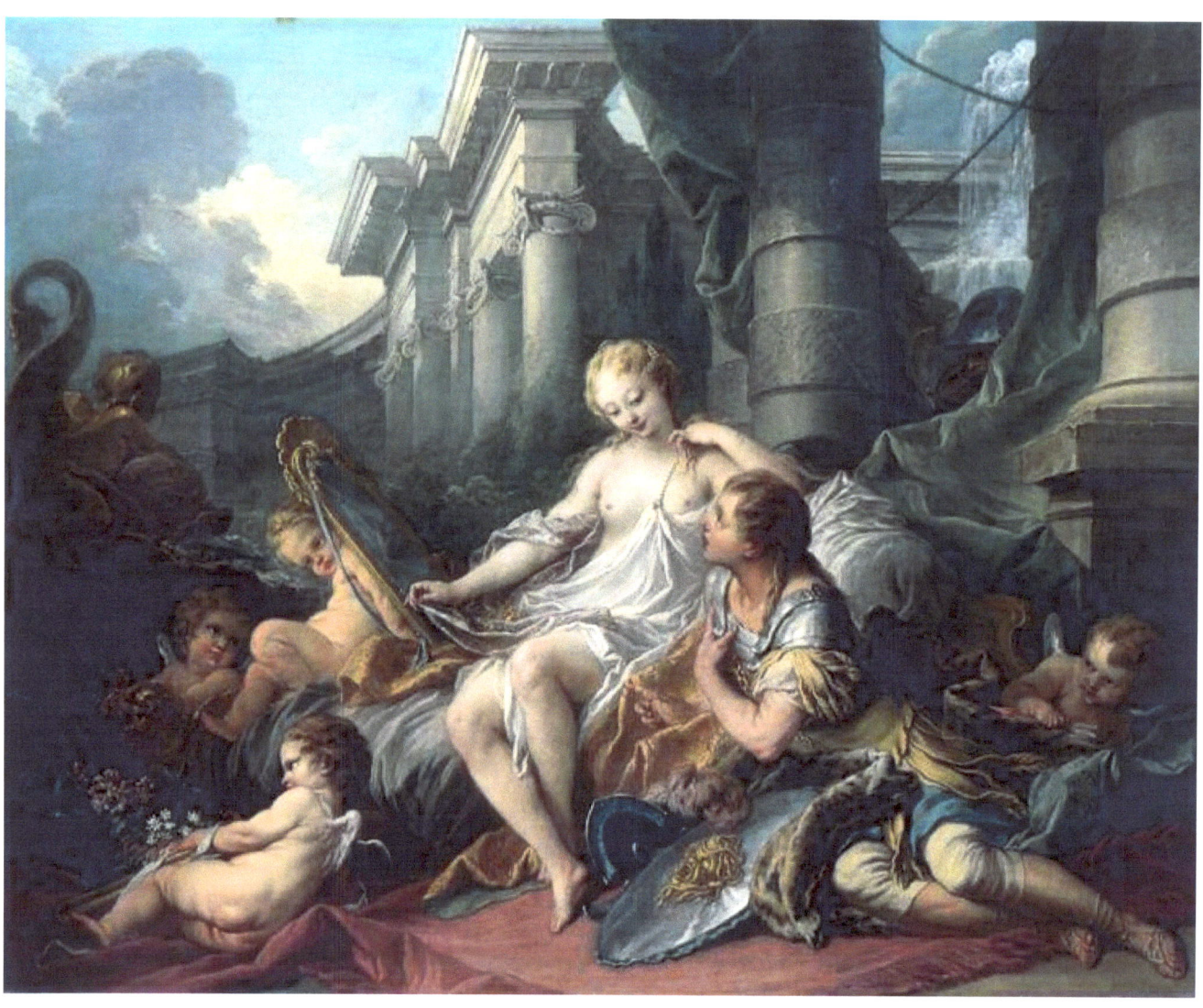

Rinaldo and Armida--Francois Boucher—1734--Rococo

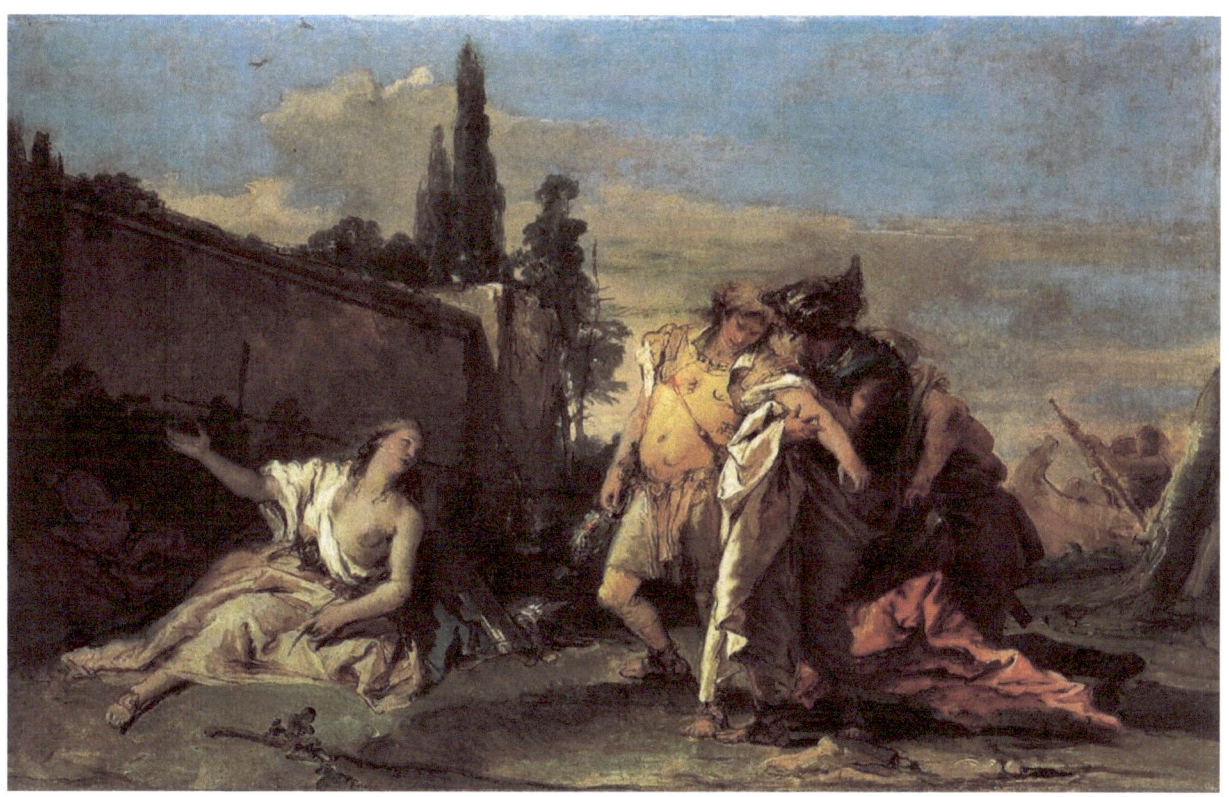

Rinaldo's Departure from Armida--Giovanni Battista Tiepolo—1760--Rococo

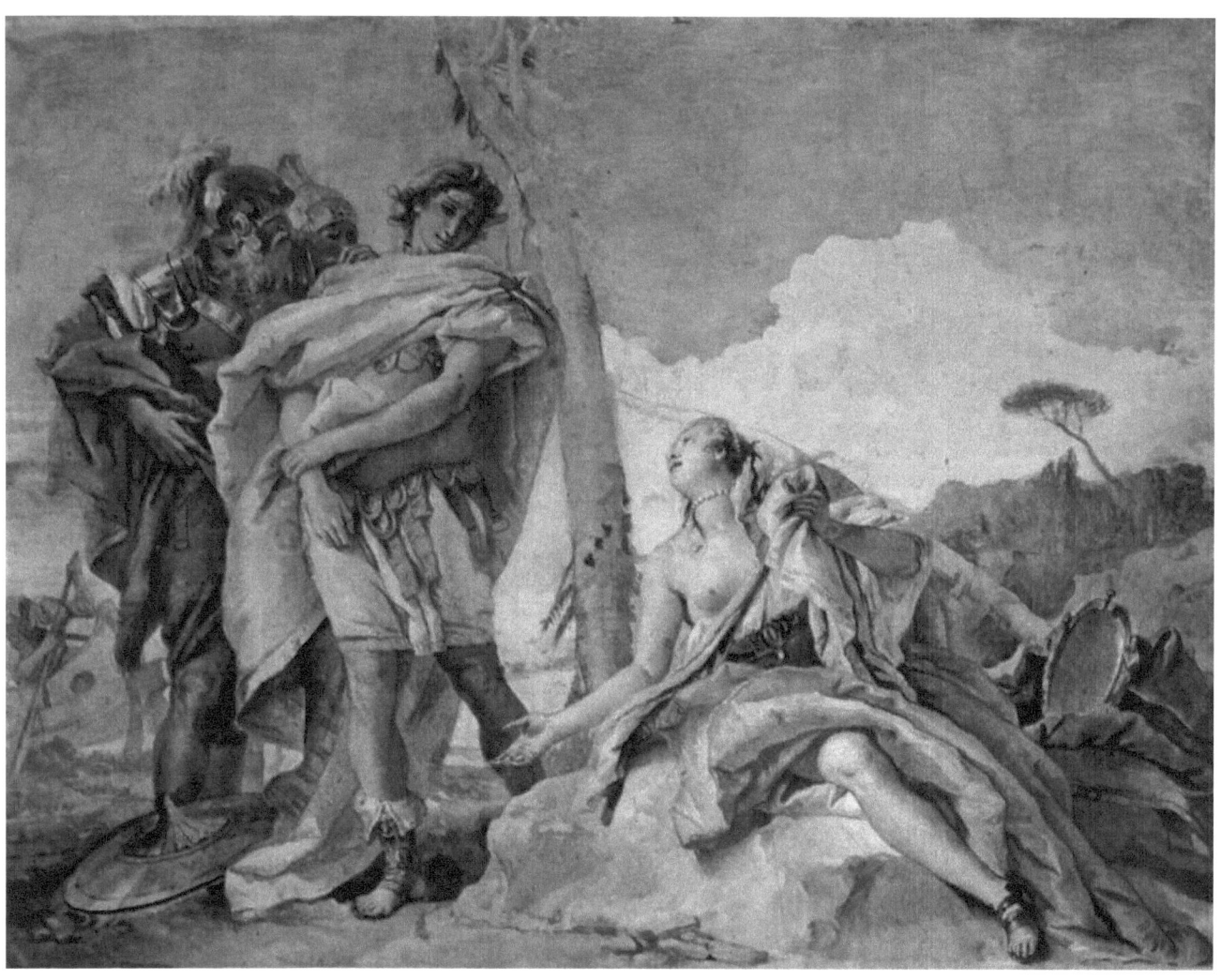

Rinaldo Abandoning Armida--Giovanni Battista Tiepolo—1757--Rococo

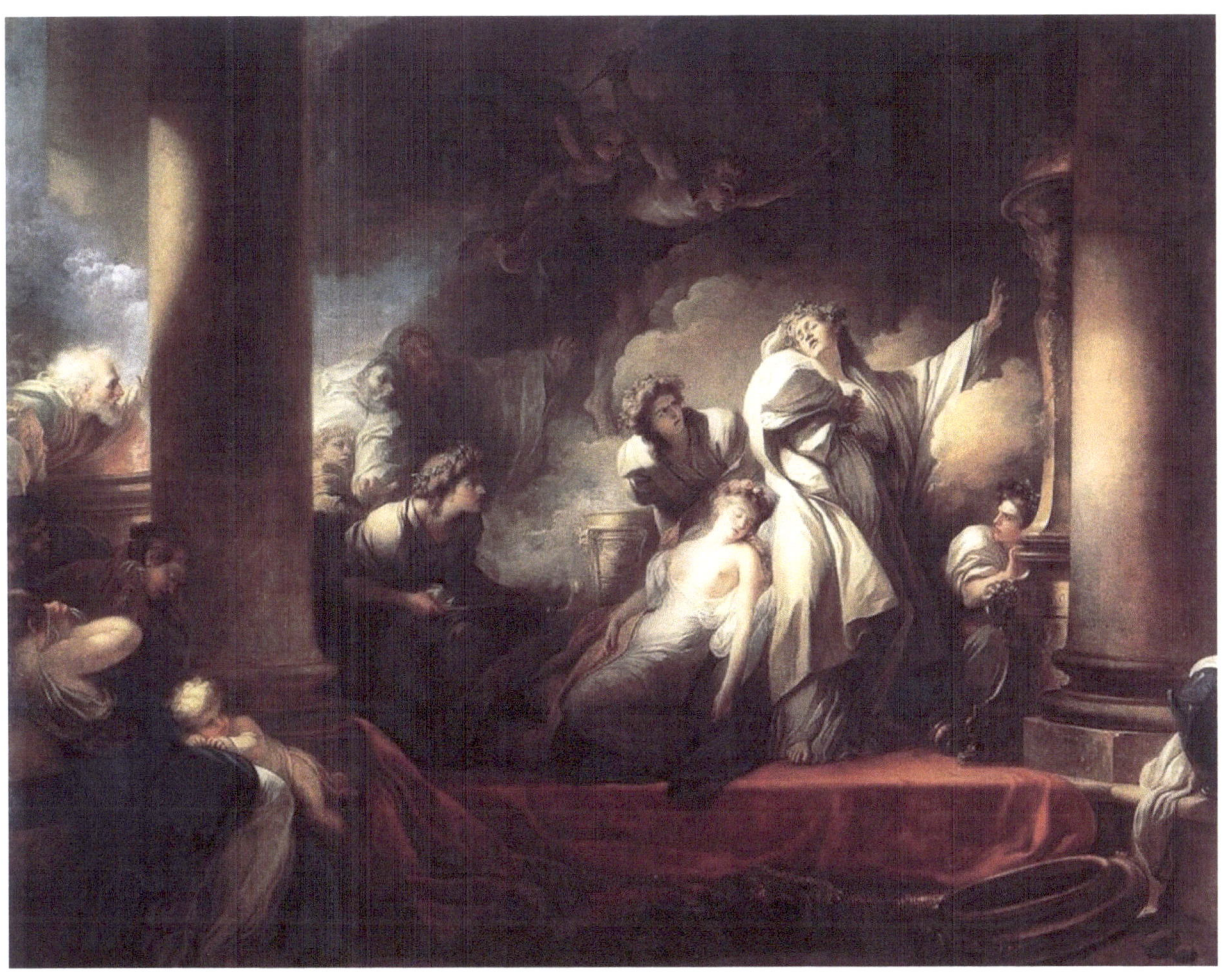

Coresus at Callirhoe--Jean-Honore Fragonard—1765--Rococo

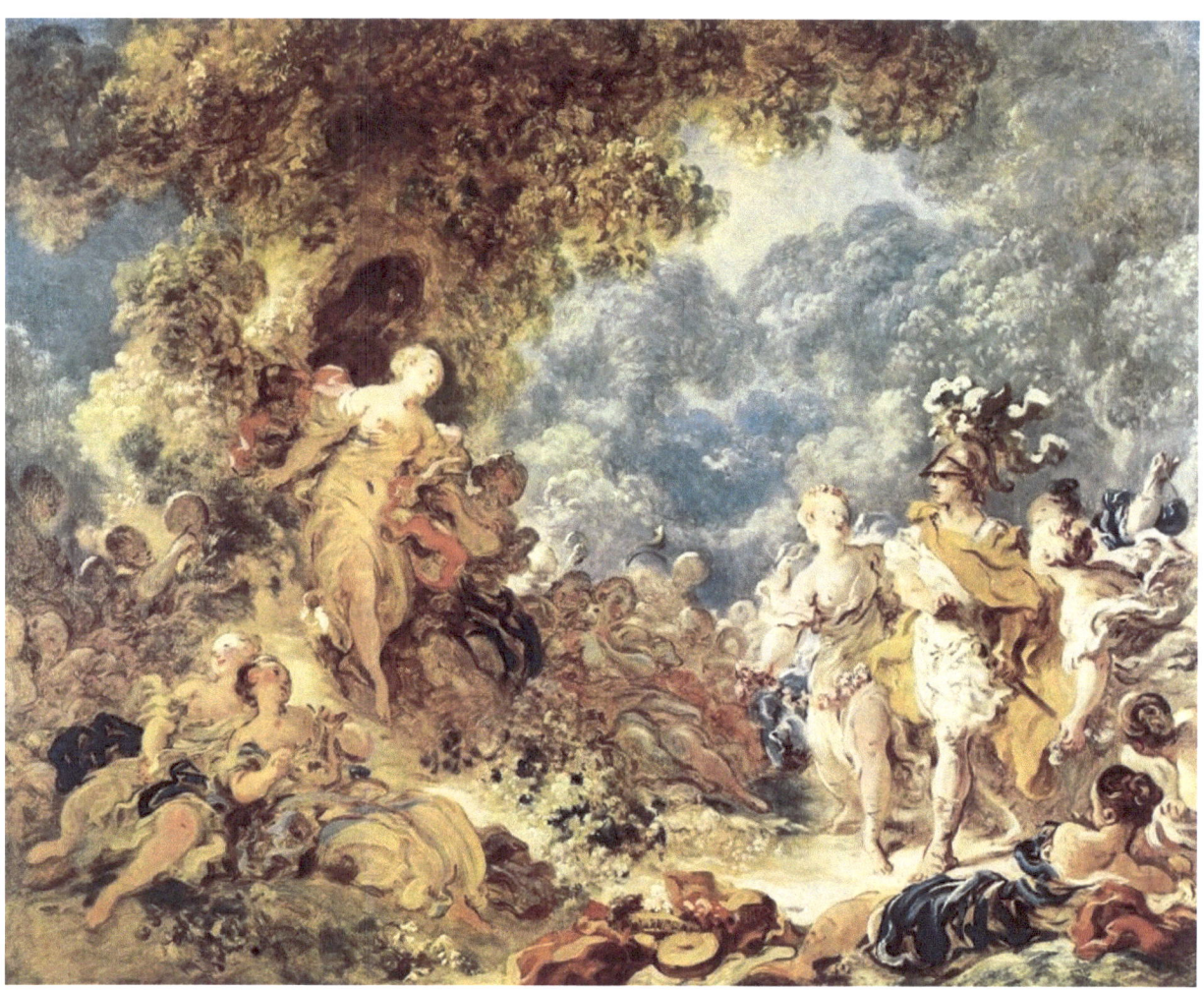

Rinaldo in the garden of the palace of Armida--Jean-Honore Fragonard--c.1763--Rococo

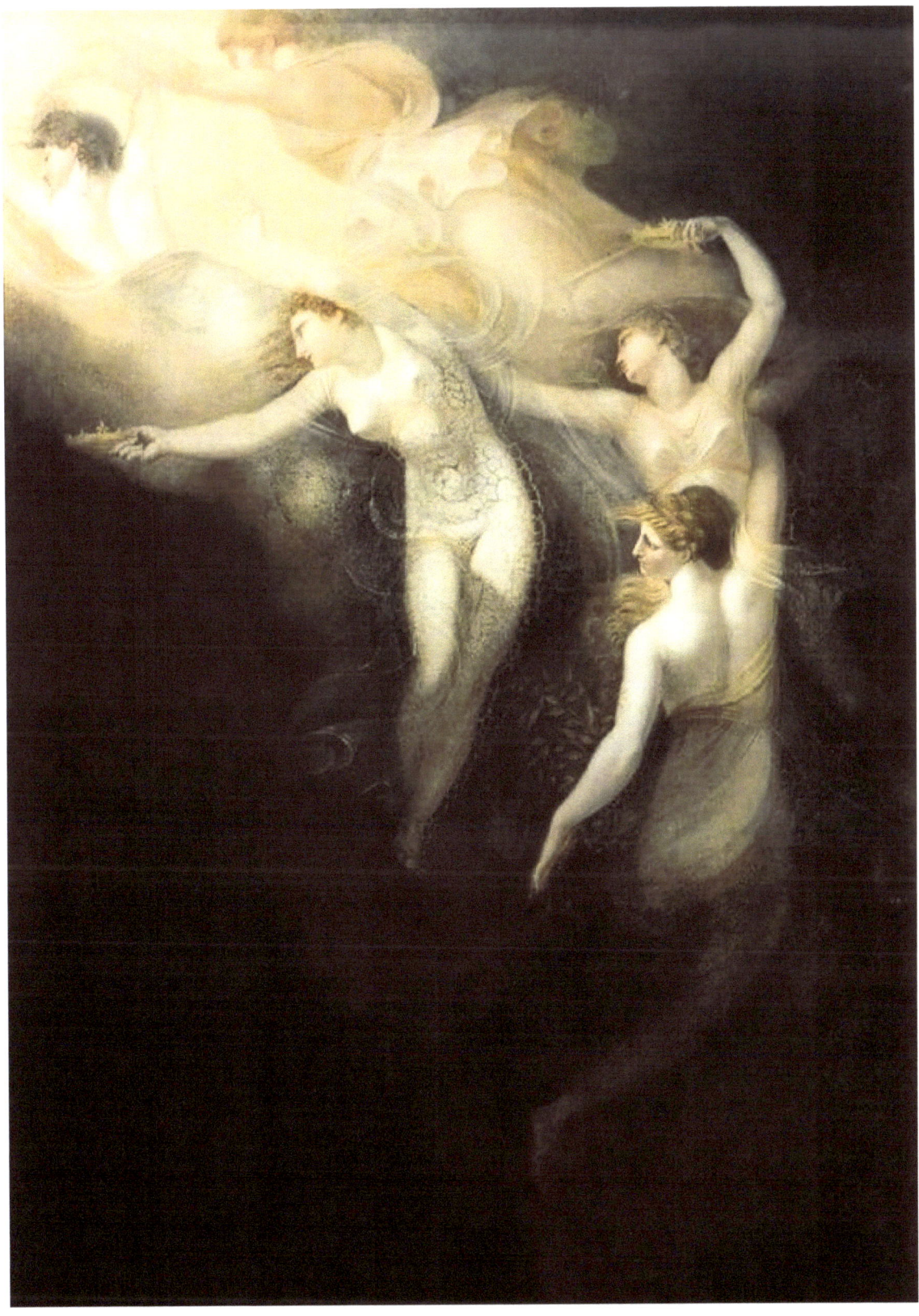

The Dream of Queen Katherine--Henry Fuseli--Romanticism

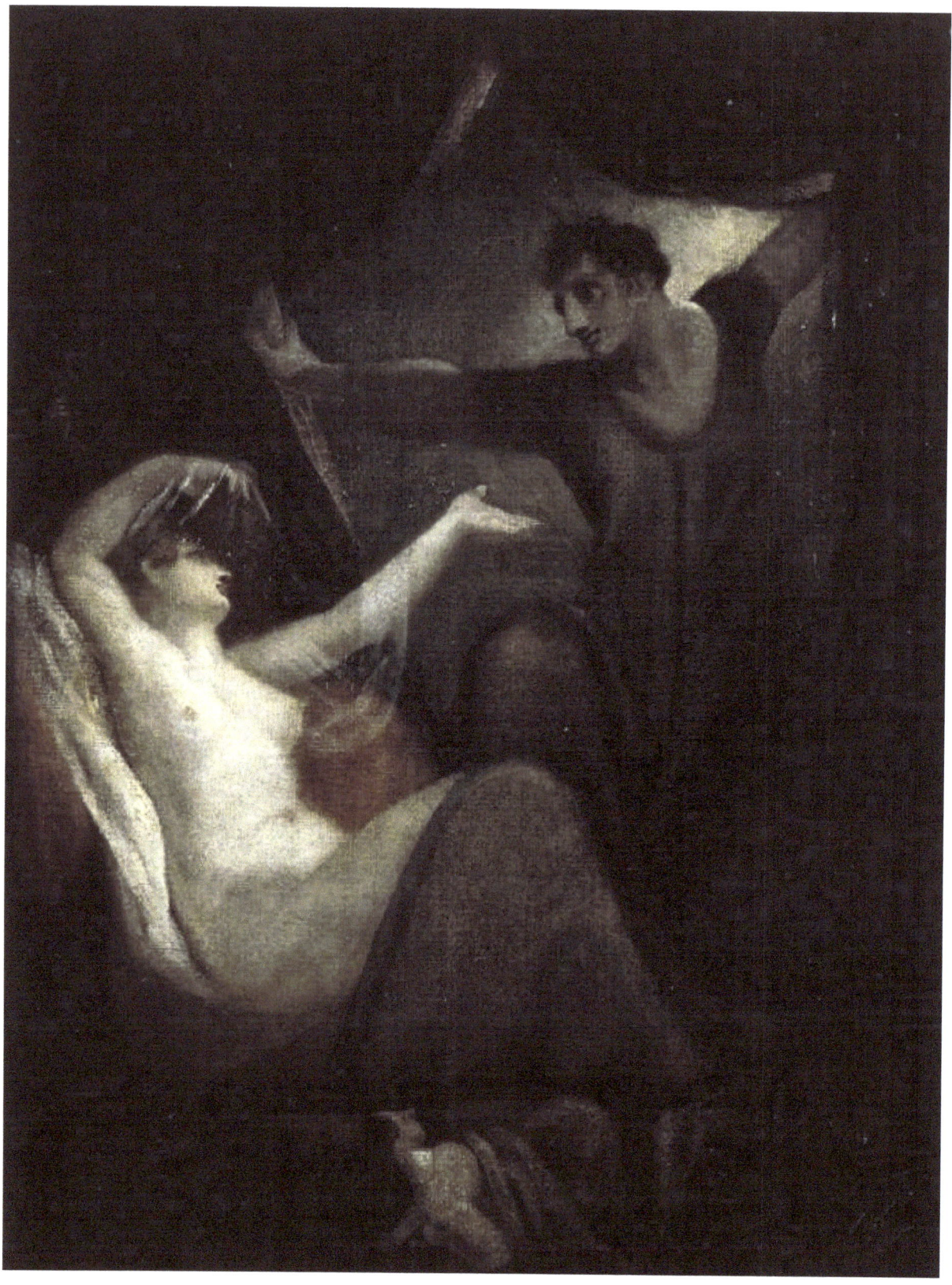

A Scene from 'The Wife of Bath's Tale'--Henry Fuseli—1812--Romanticism

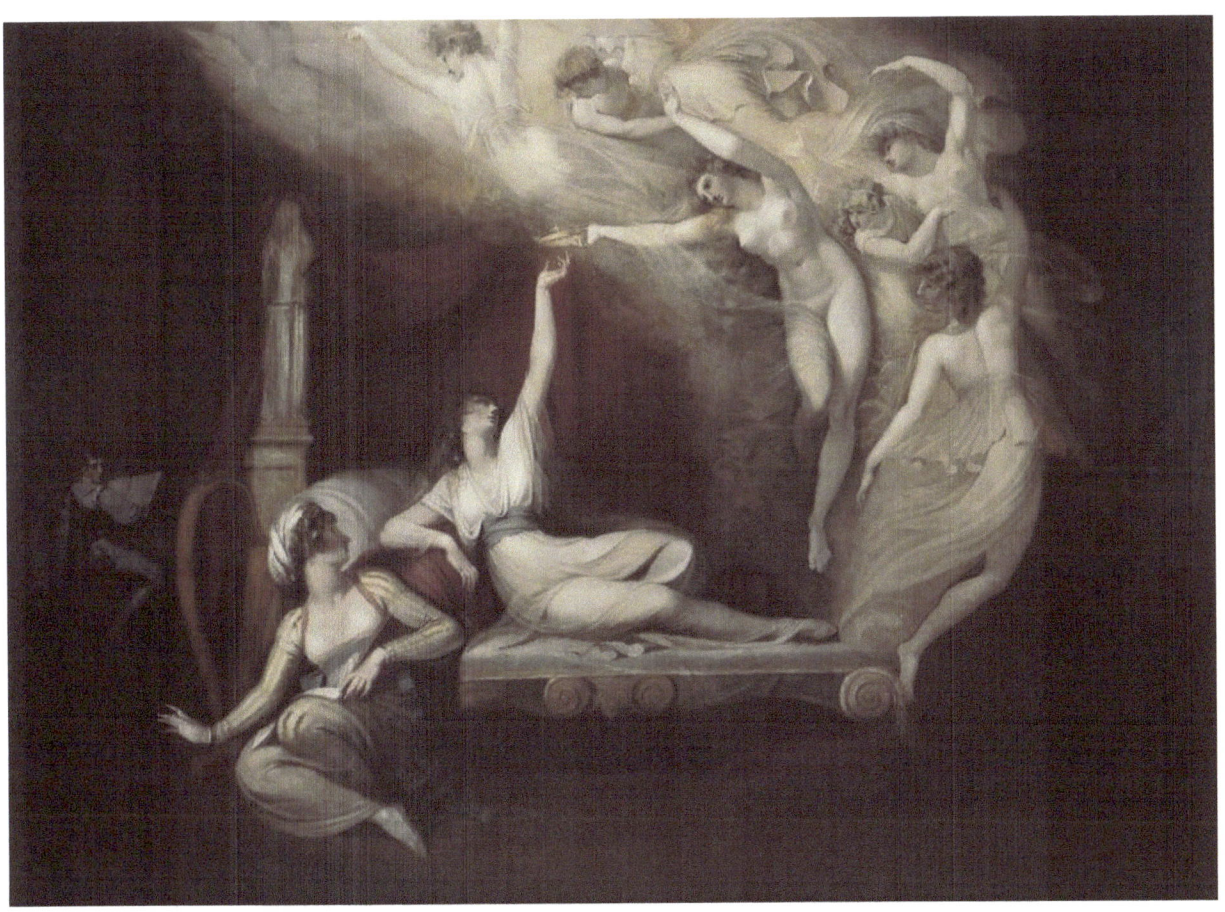

The Vision of Catherine of Aragon-- Henry Fuseli--Romanticism

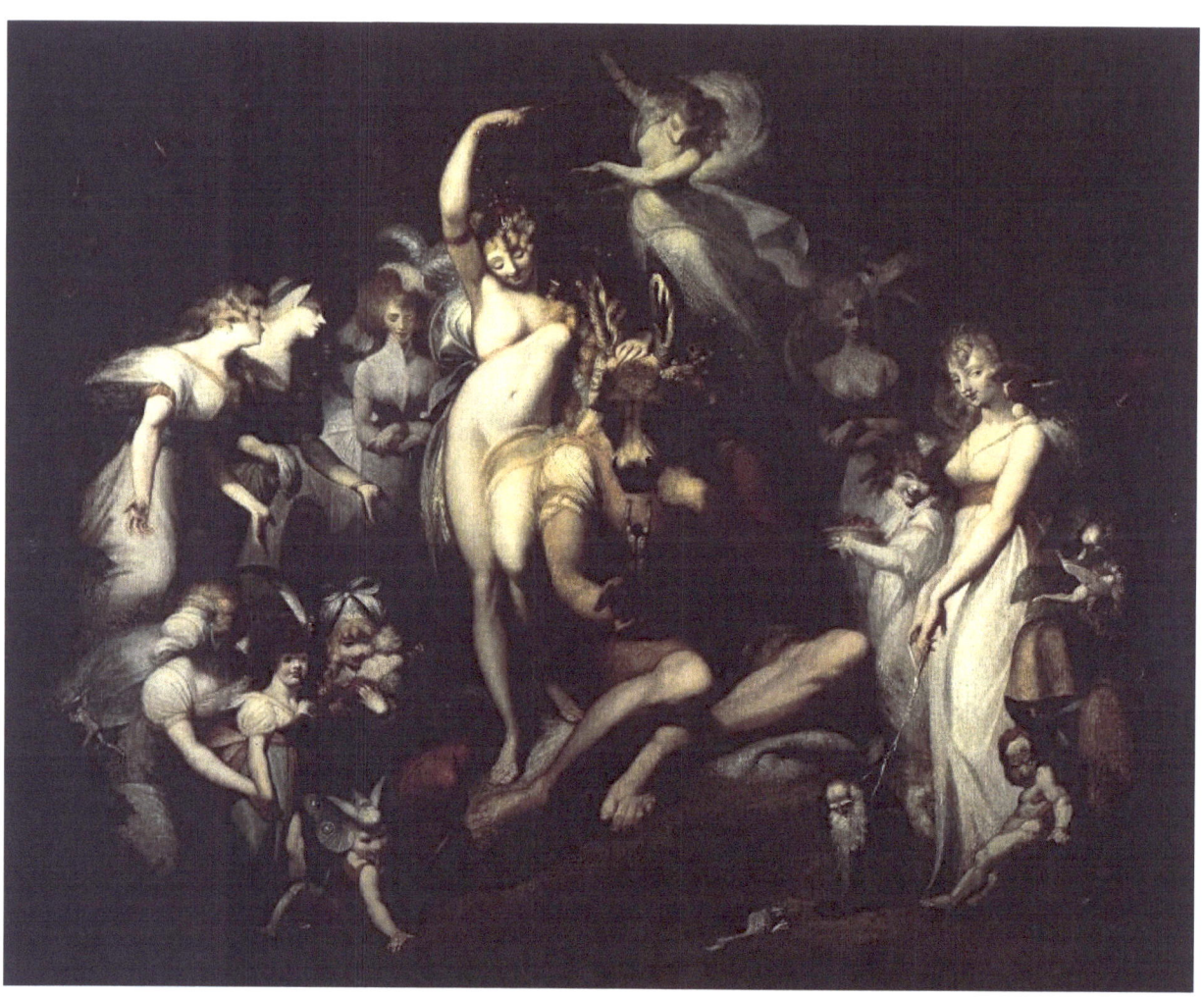

Titania and Bottom--Henry Fuseli—1790--Romanticism

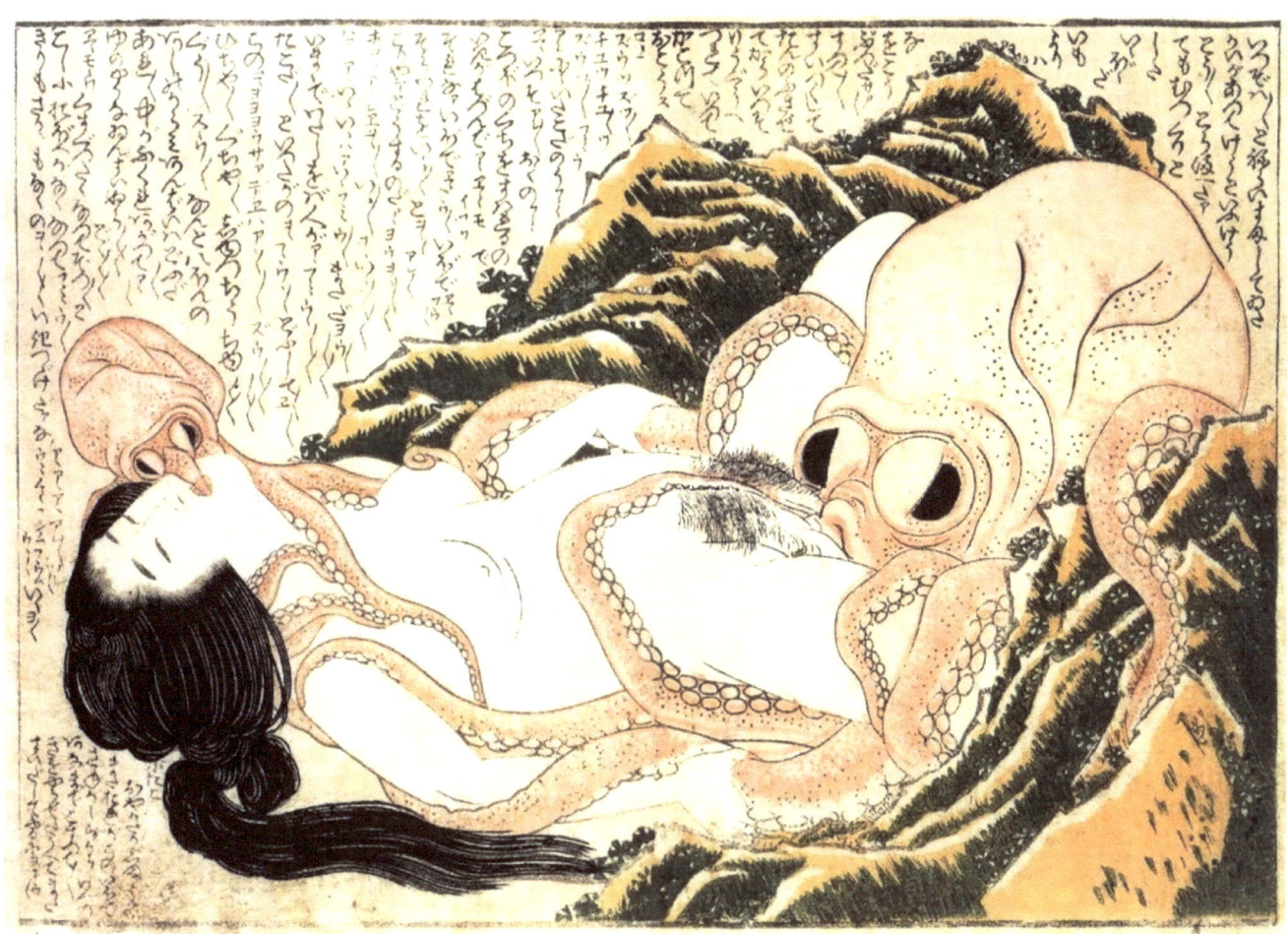

The Dream of the Fisherman's Wife-- Katsushika Hokusai—1814--Ukiyo-e

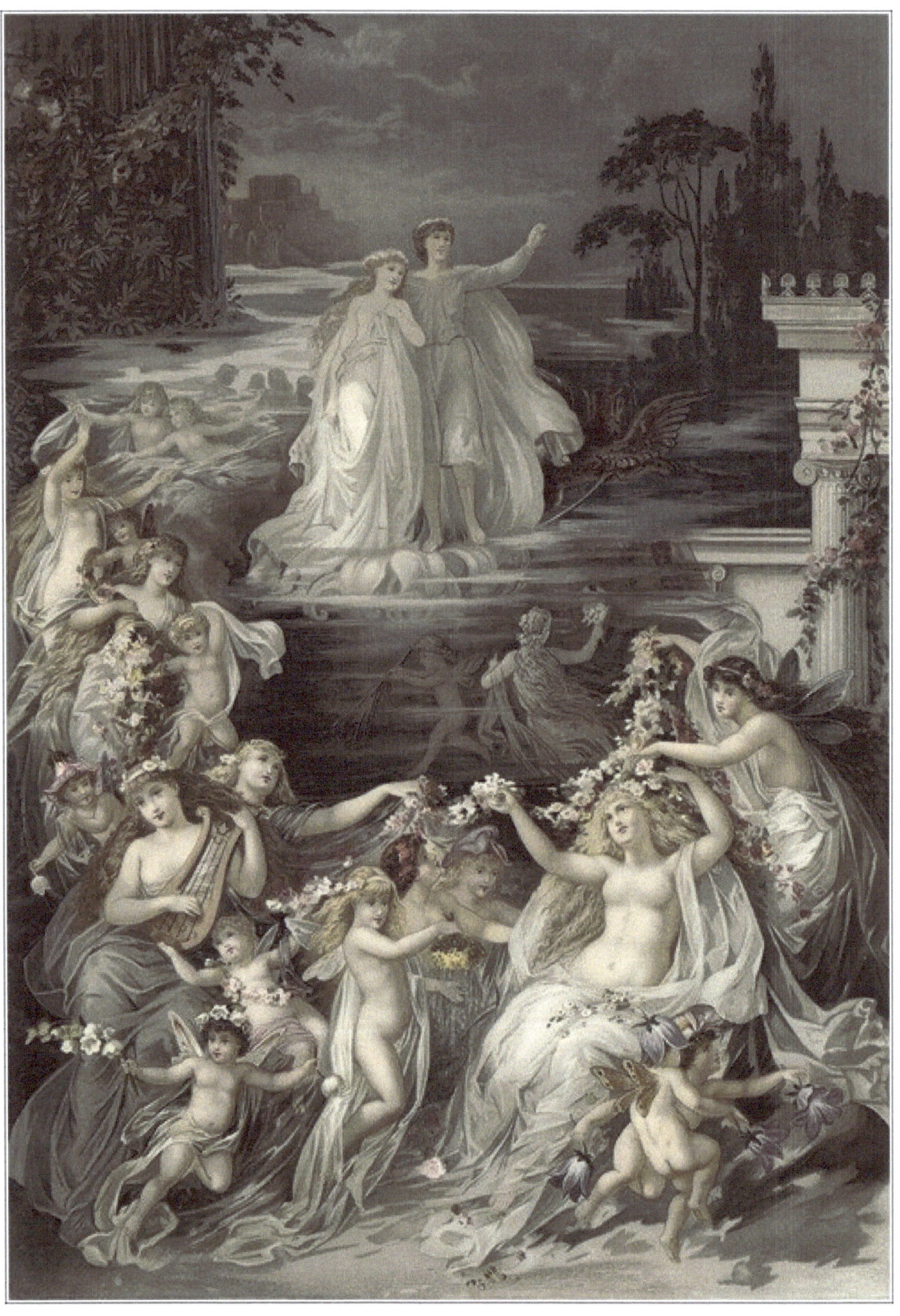

Midsummer night's dream--John Hoppner--Romanticism

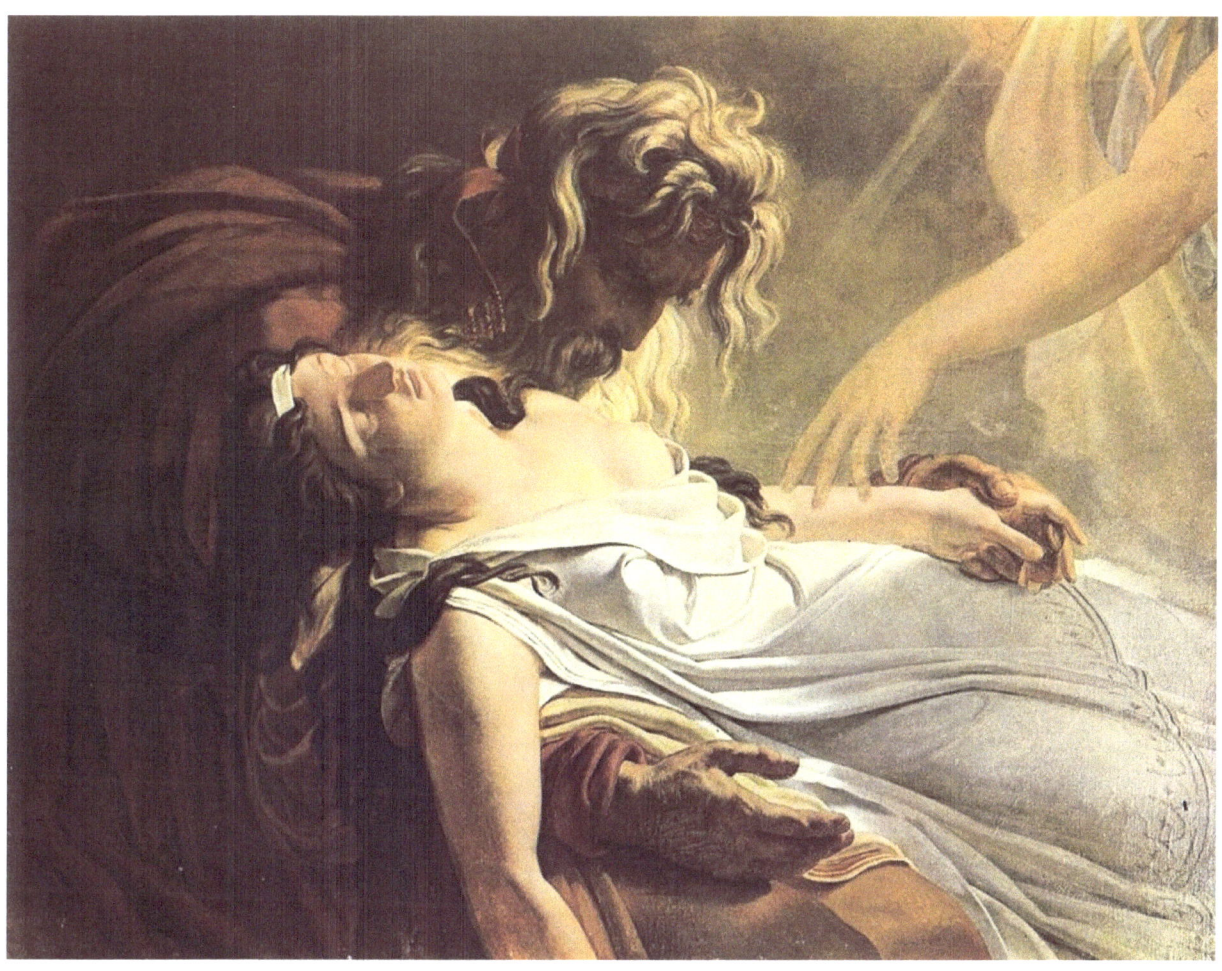

 Malvine, Dying in the Arms of Fingal--Anne-Louis Girodet--Neoclassicism, Romanticism

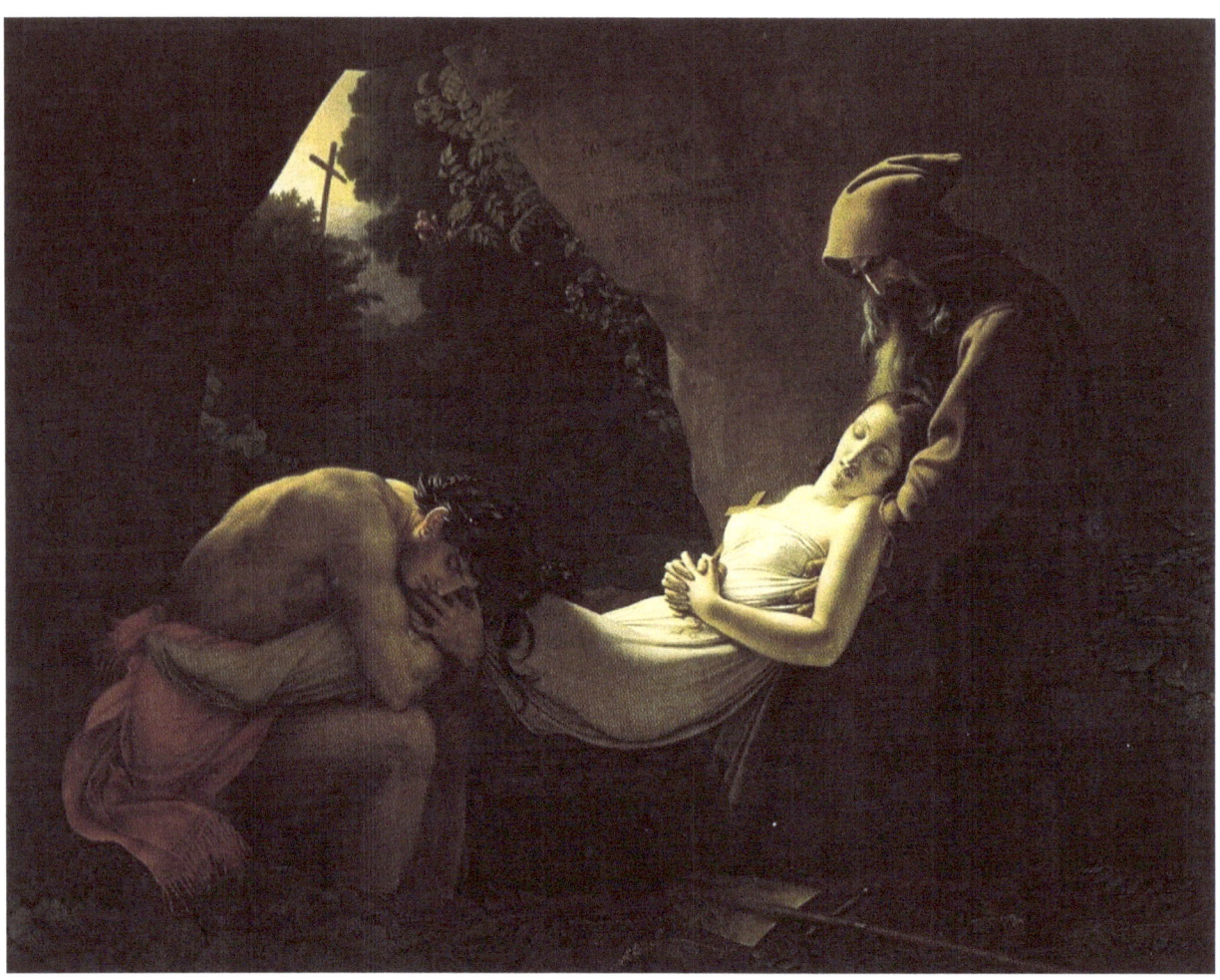

The Burial of Atala-- Anne-Louis Girodet—1808--Romanticism

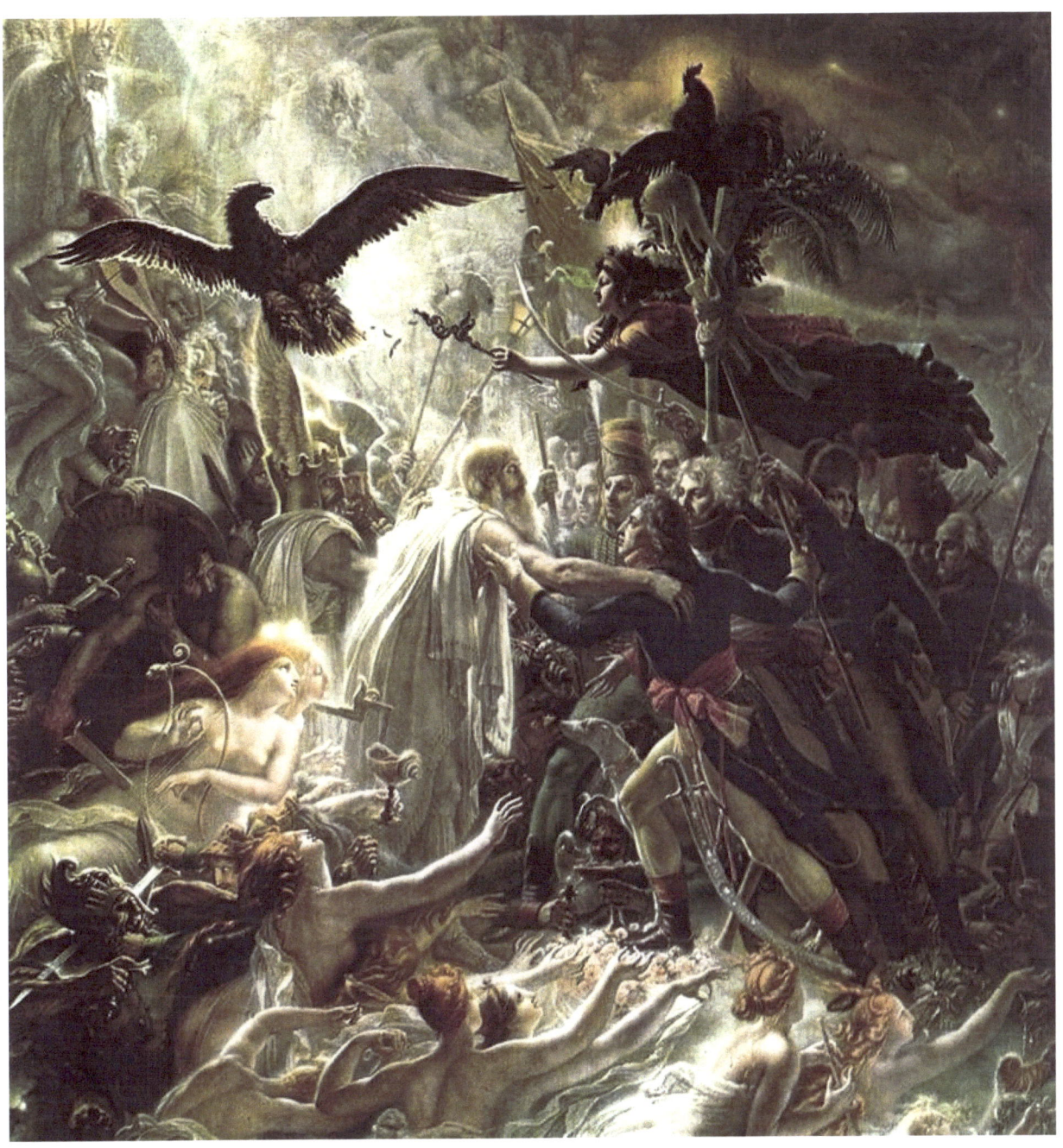

Malvine, Dying in the Arms of Fingal--Anne-Louis Girodet--
Neoclassicism, Romanticism

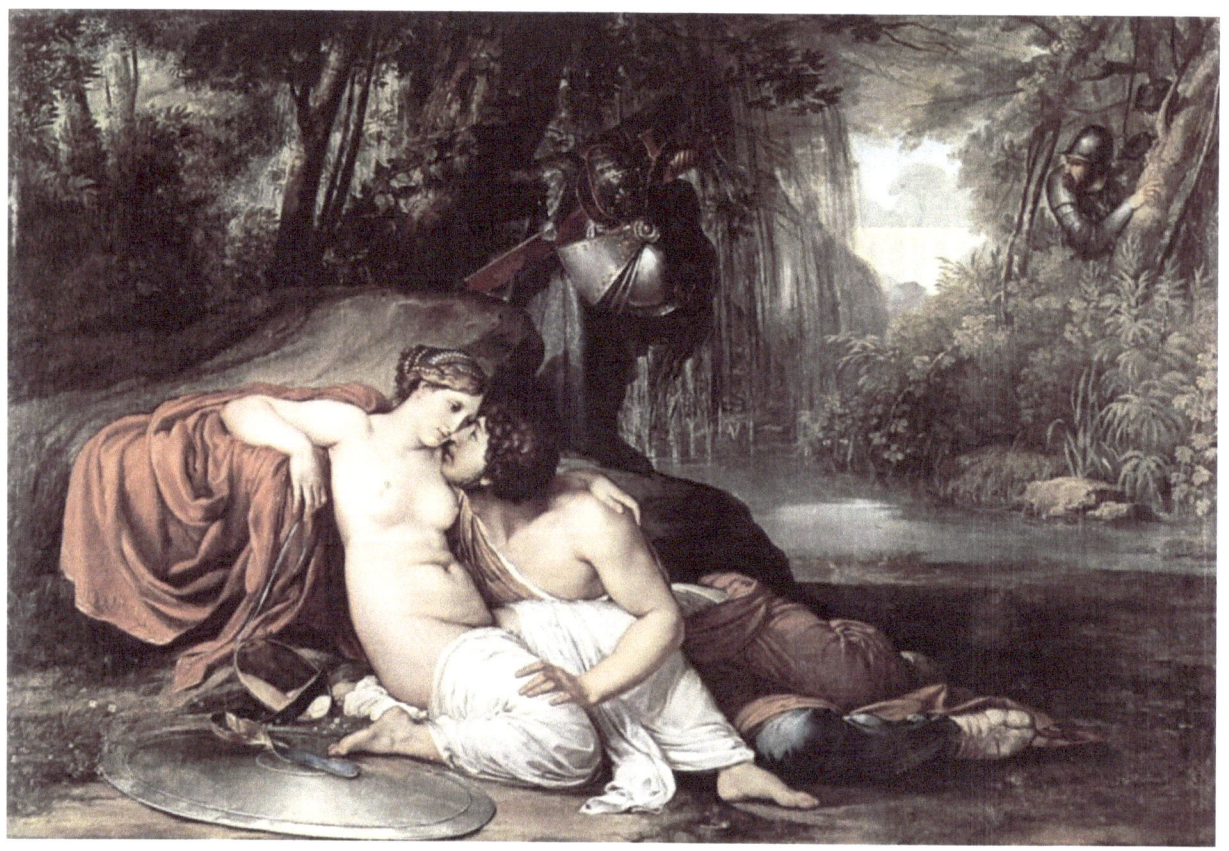

Rinaldo and Armida-- Francesco Hayez—Italy--Romanticism

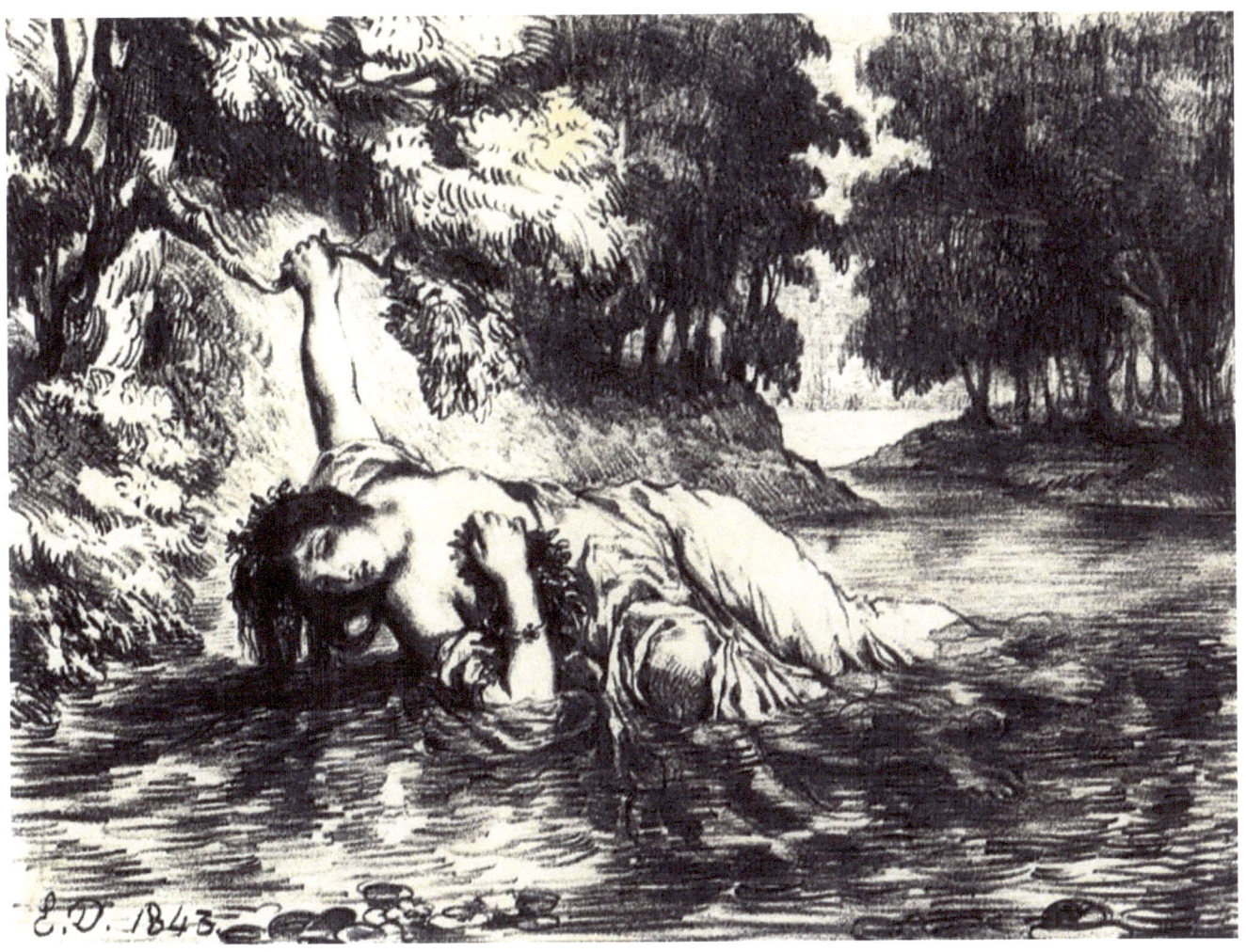

The Death of Ophelia--Eugene Delacroix—1843--Romanticism

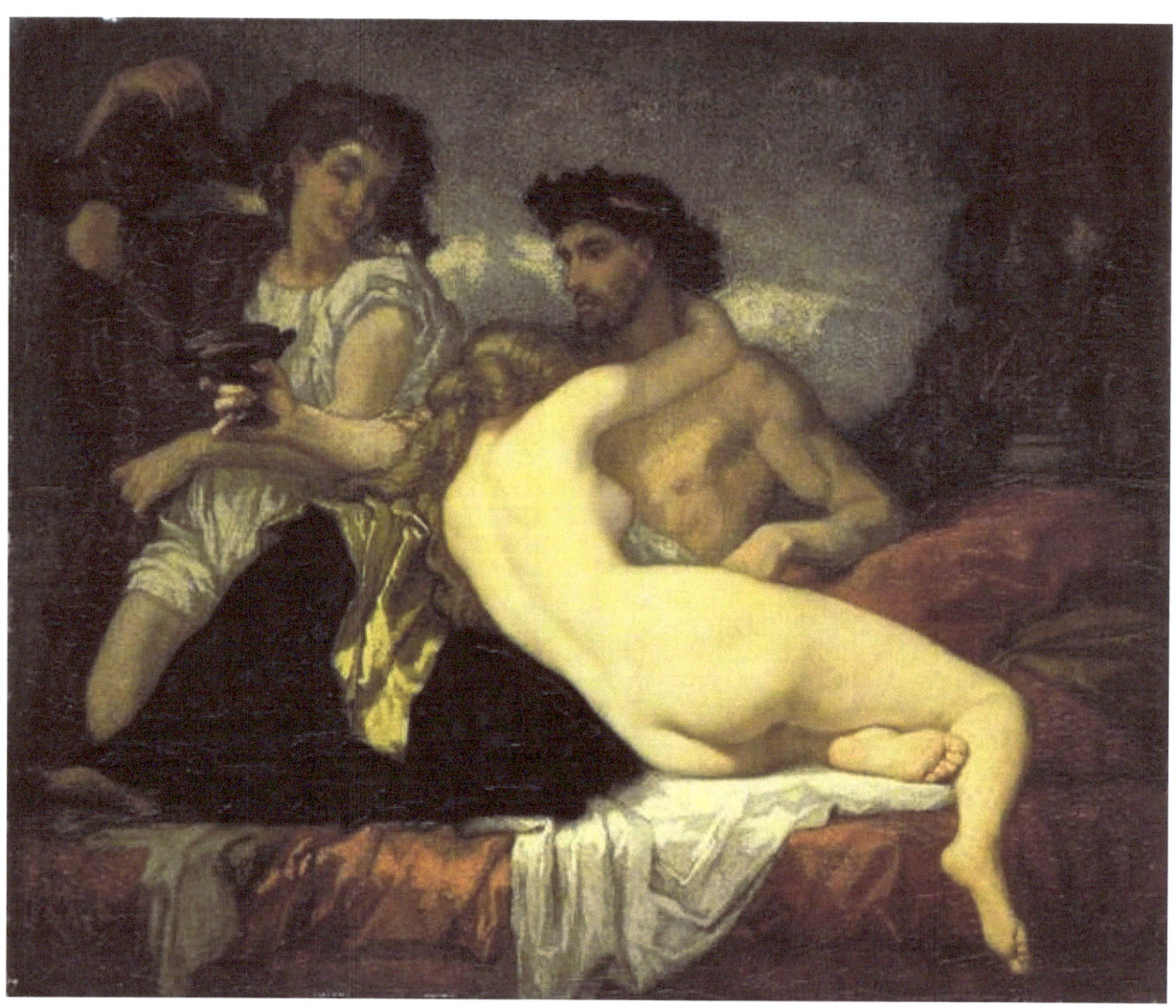

Horace and Lydia--Thomas Couture—1843--Academicism

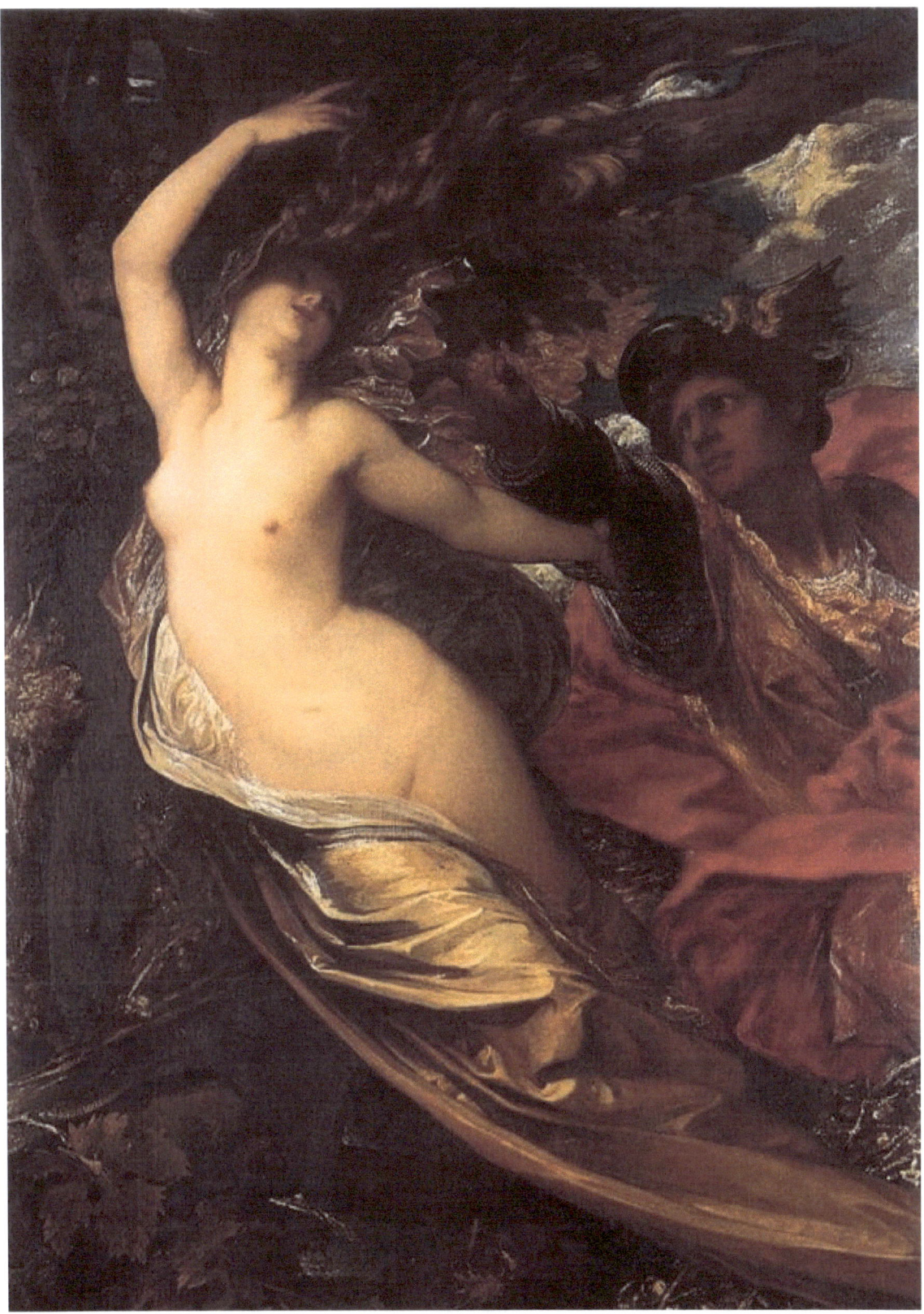

Orlando Pursuing the Fata Morgana--George Frederick Watts—1848--Academicism

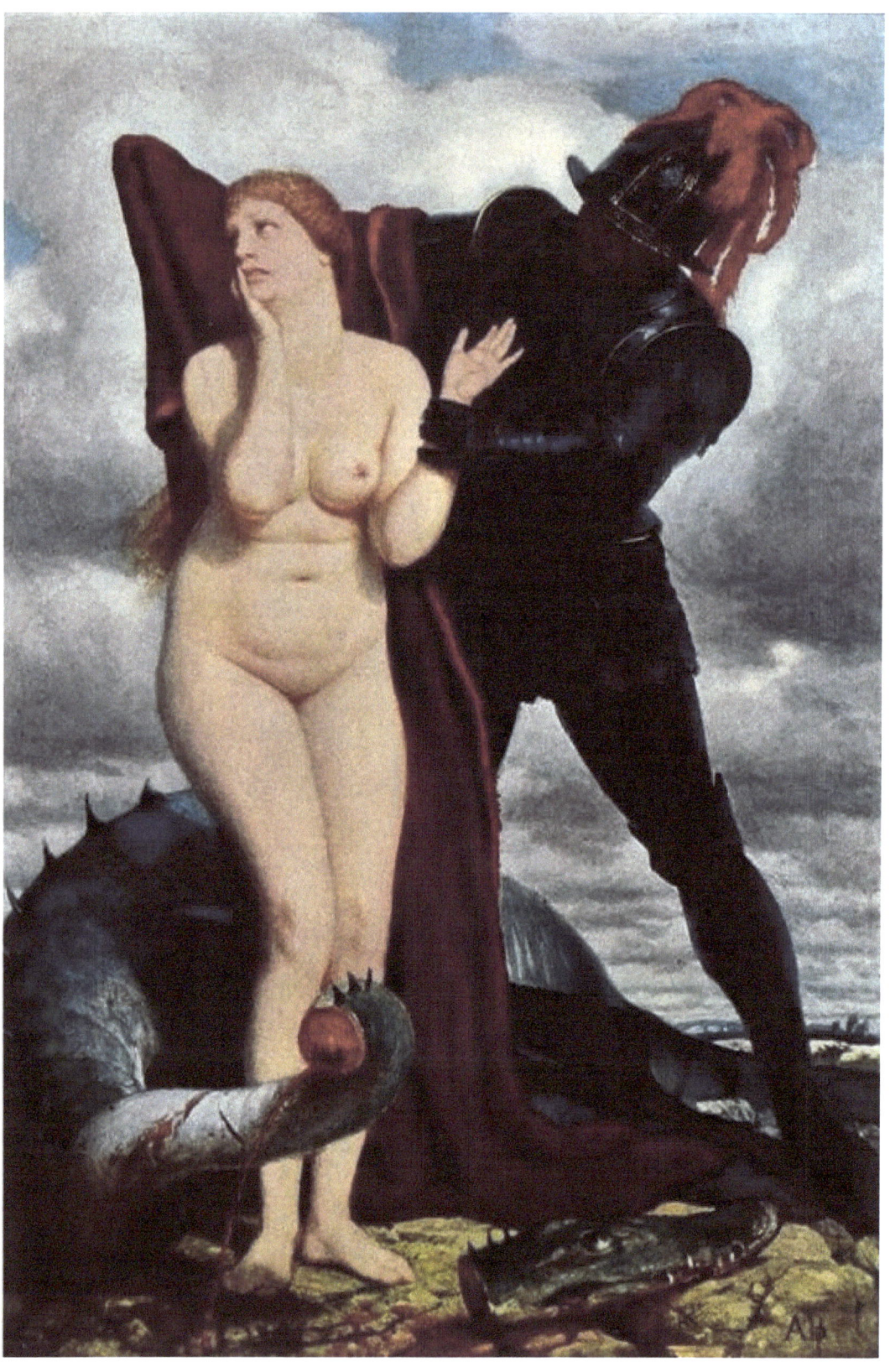

Angelika, guarded by a dragon-- Arnold Böcklin-- c.1880--Symbolism

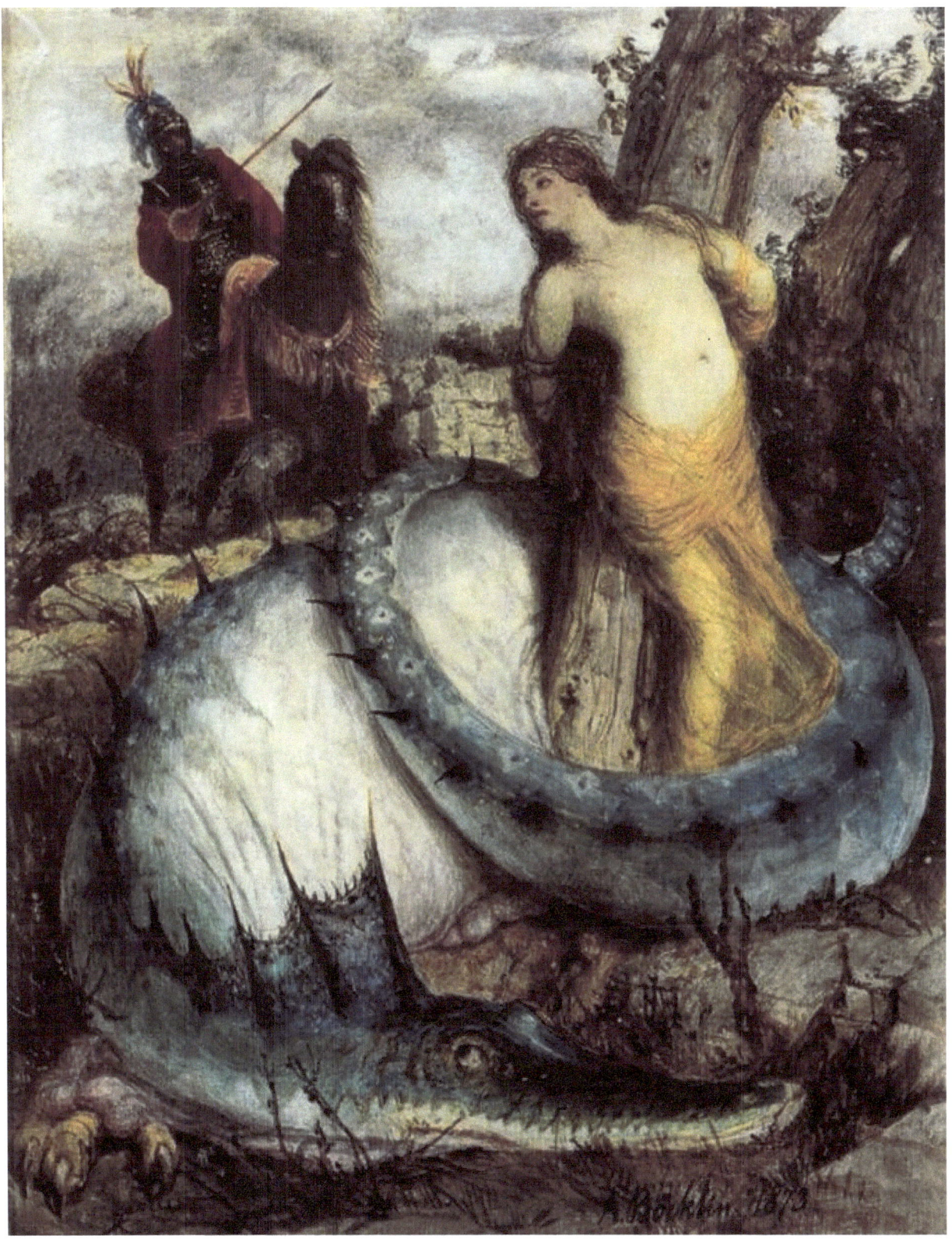

Angelika, guarded by a dragon (Angelica and Ruggiero)--Arnold Böcklin--c.1872--Symbolism

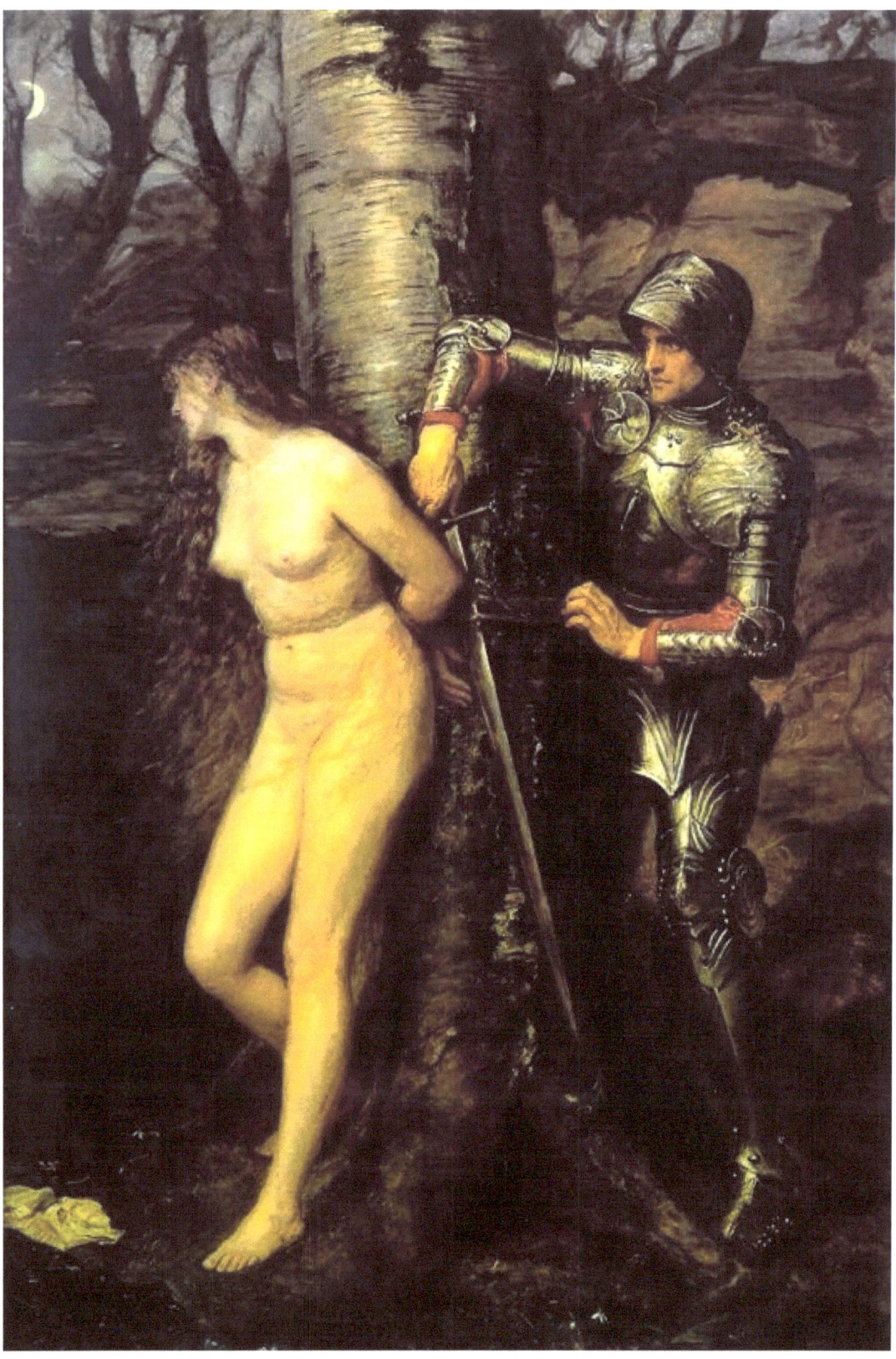

The Knight Errant-- John Everett Millais—1870--Romanticism

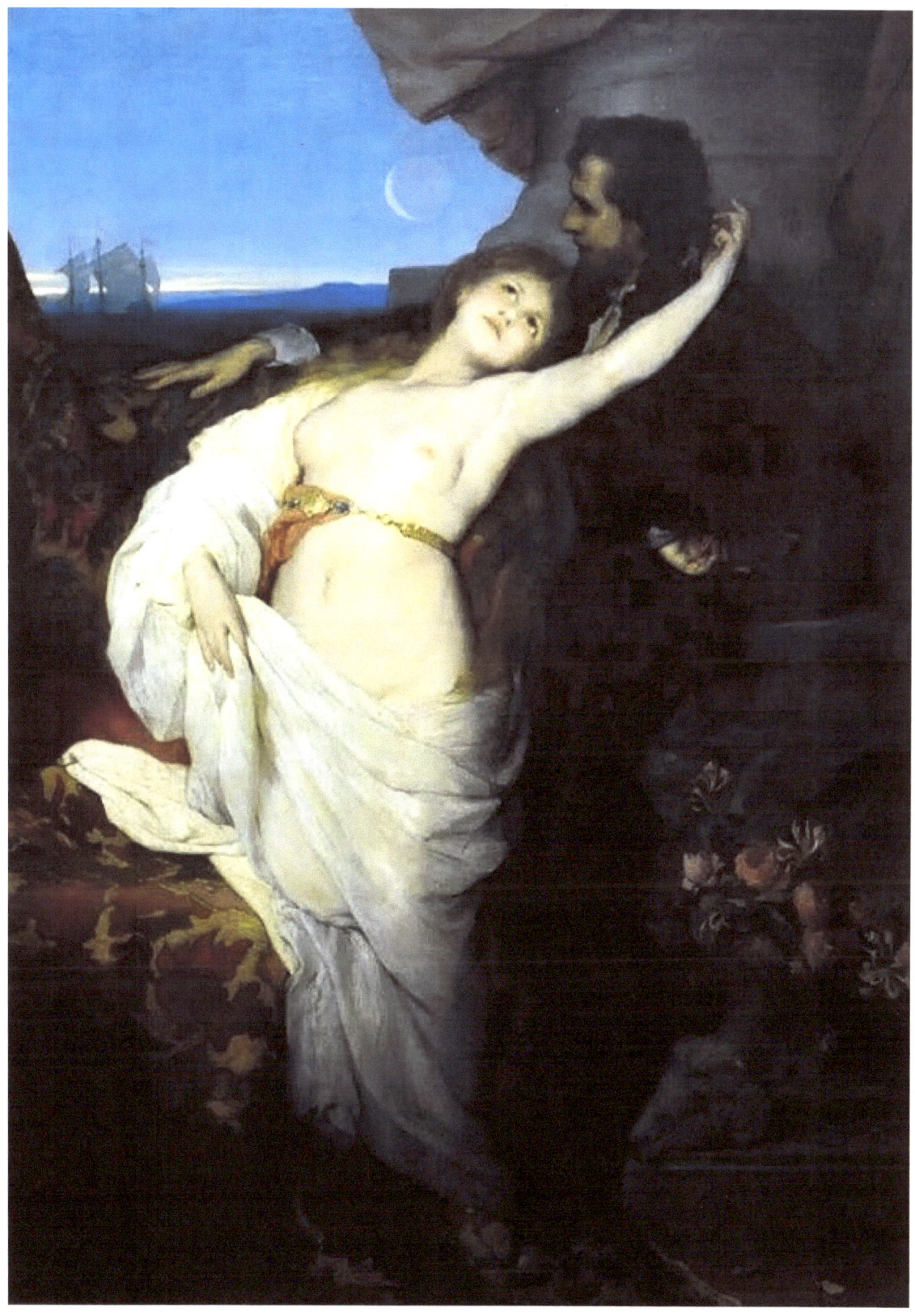

Tannhäuser-- Gabriel von Max—1878--Symbolism

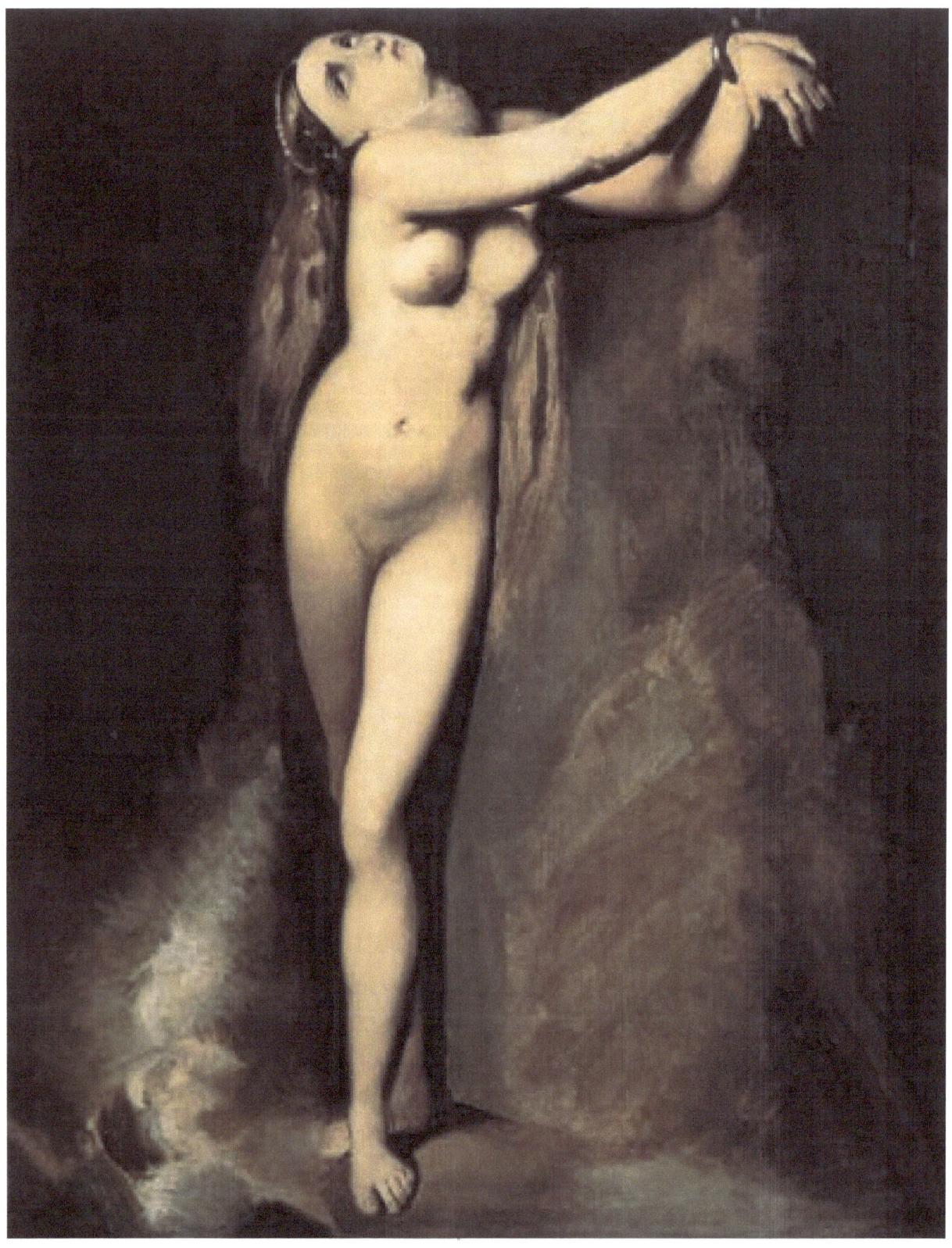

Angelica at the rock (After ingres)--Georges Seurat—1878--Neoclassicism

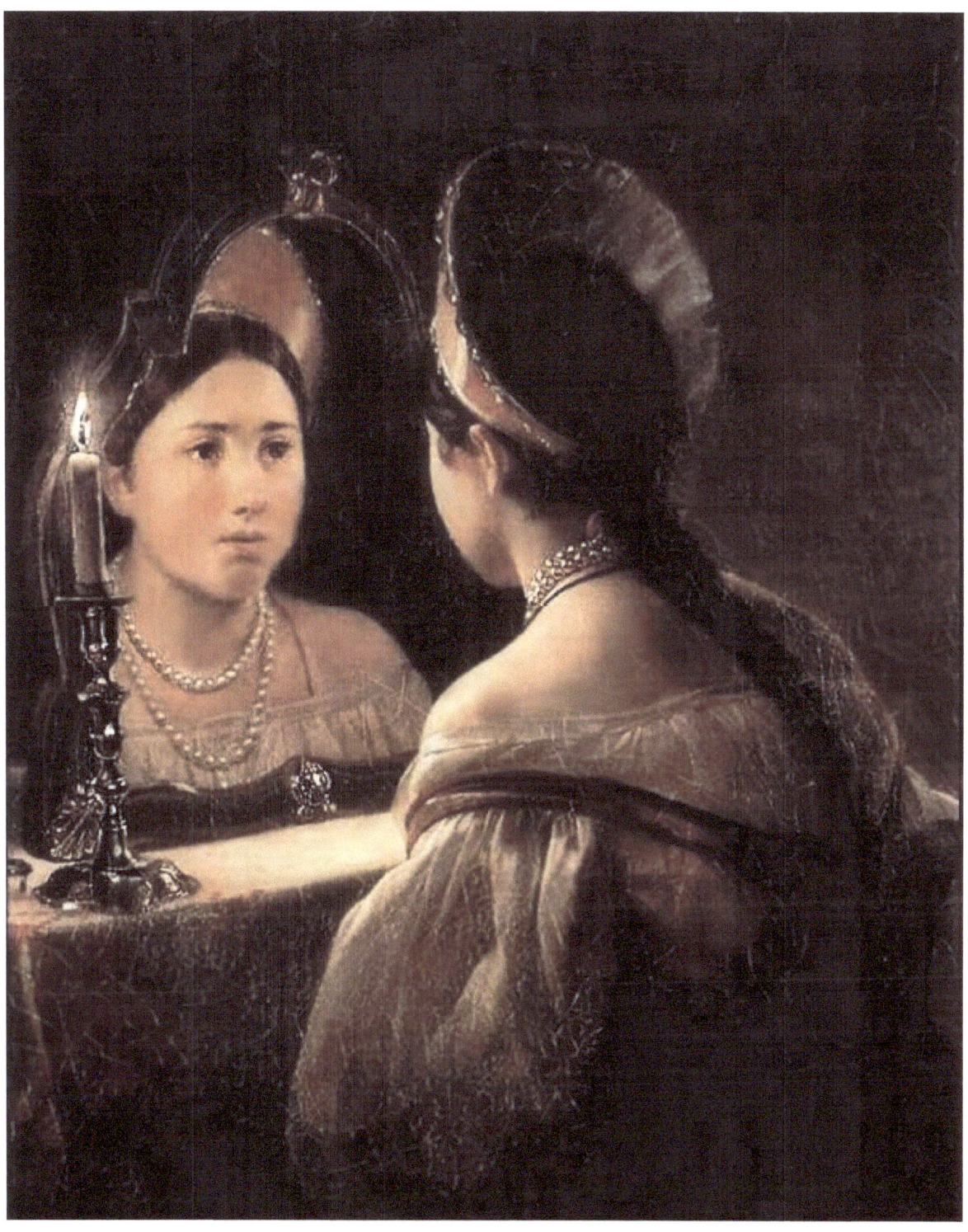

Erminia and the Shepherds-- Karl Bryullov—1824--Romanticism

Édouard-Henri Avril, 1843–1928 (pseudonym Paul Avril)-- Born in Algiers-- was a French erotic artist who is best known for his paintings and illustrations for various erotic novels.

Édouard-Henri Avril major work was designs for *De Figuris Veneris: A Manual of Classical Erotica* by the German scholar Friedrich Karl Forberg. However, he also illustrated such works as Gustave Flaubert's *Salammbô*, Gautier's *Le Roi Caundale*, John Cleland's *Fanny Hill*, Jean Baptiste Louvet de Couvray's *Adventures of the Chevalier de Faublas*, Mario Uchard's *Mon Oncle Barbassou* (scenes in a harem), Jules Michelet's *The Madam*, Hector France's *Musk, Hashish and Blood*, the writings of Pietro Aretino, and the anonymous lesbian novel *Gamiani*.

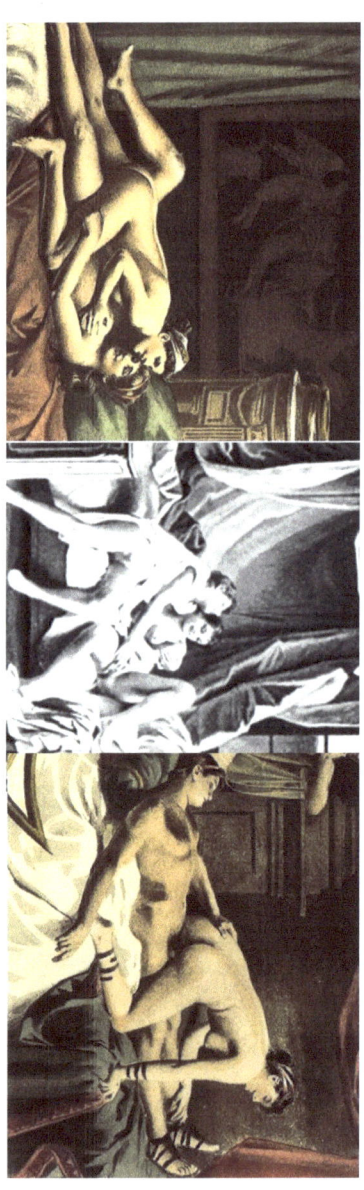

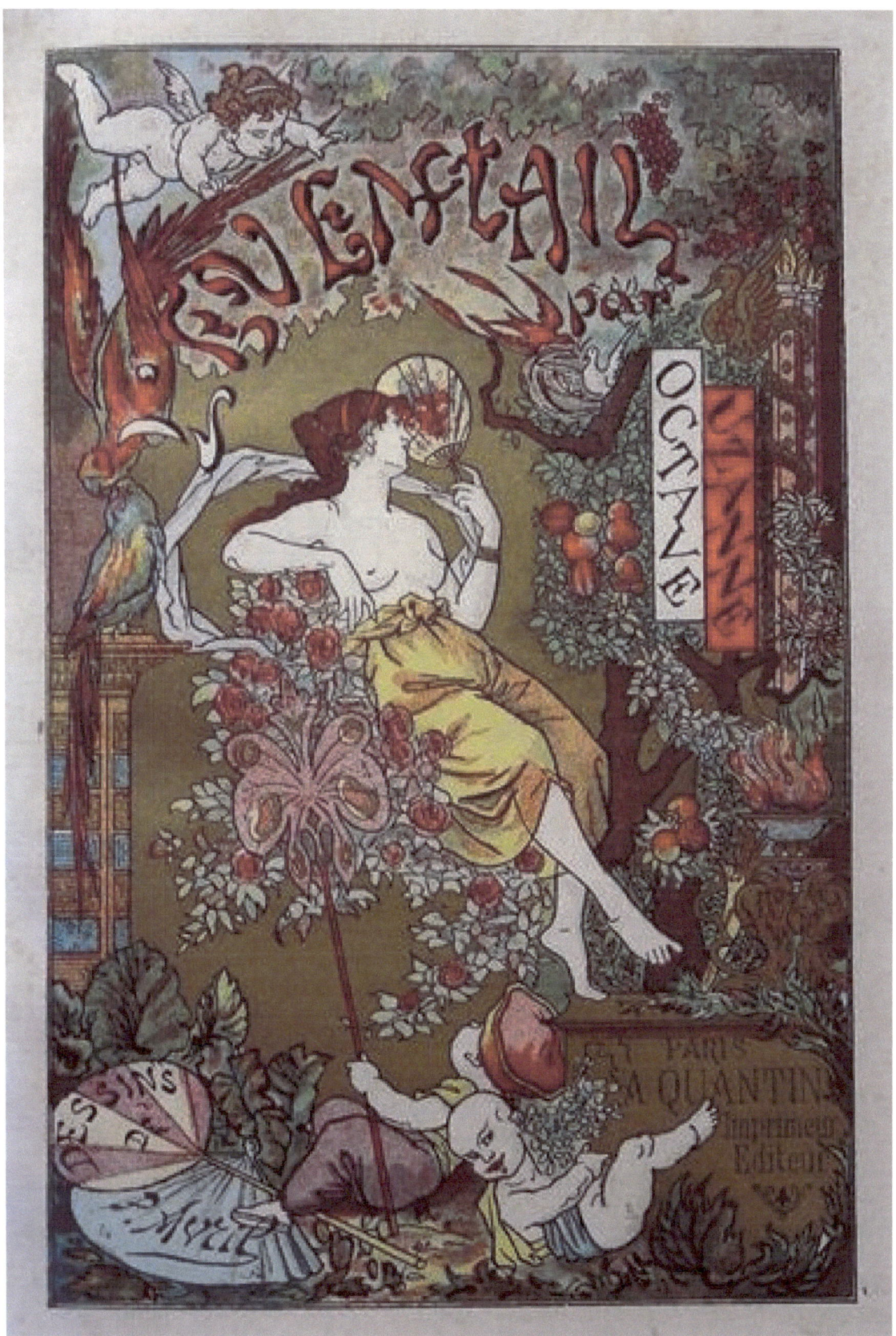

Octave Uzanne: *L'Éventail*, Paris, Quantin 1882--Cover

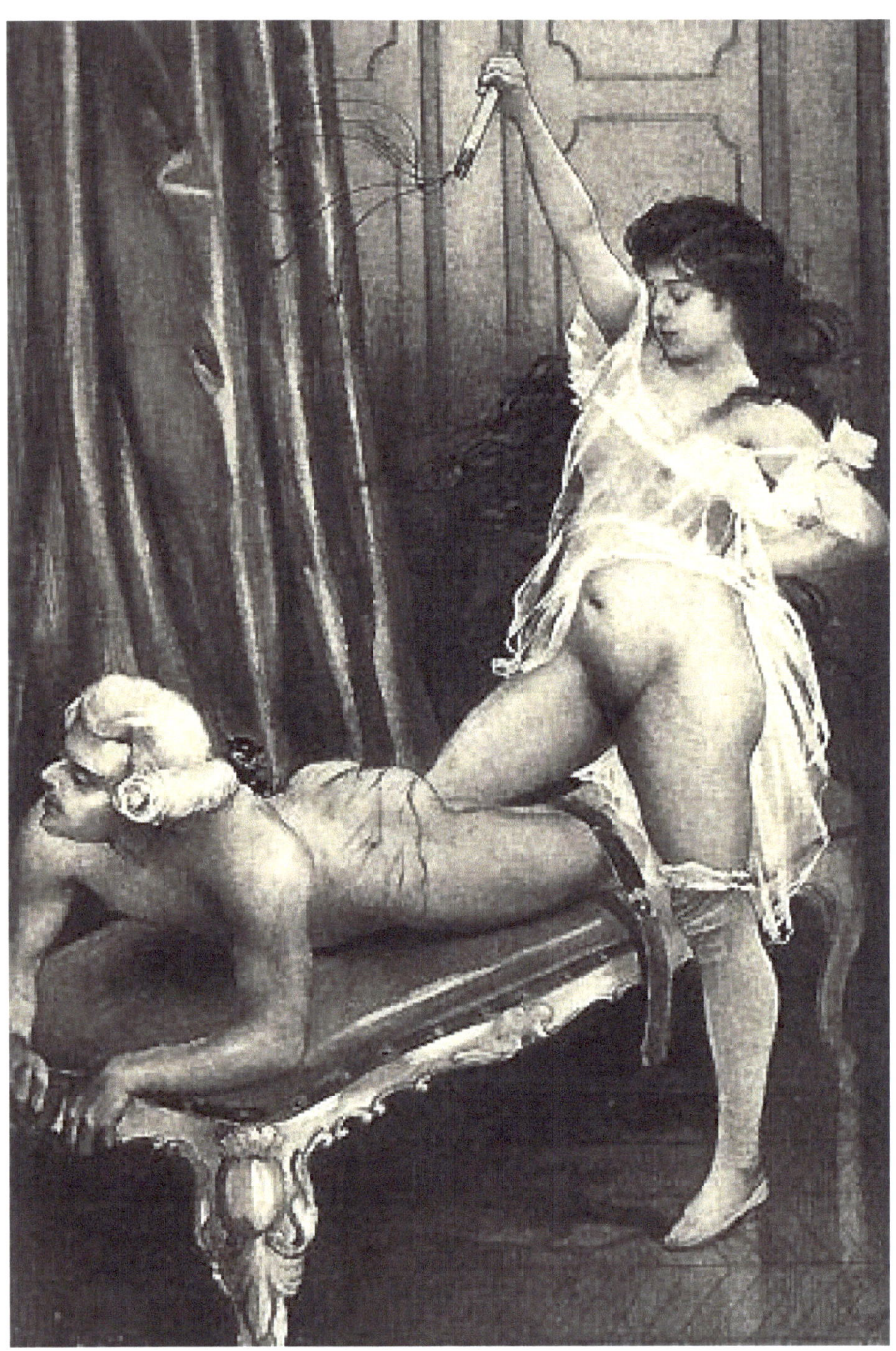

Fanny whips Mr. Barville in *Fanny Hill* by John Cleland

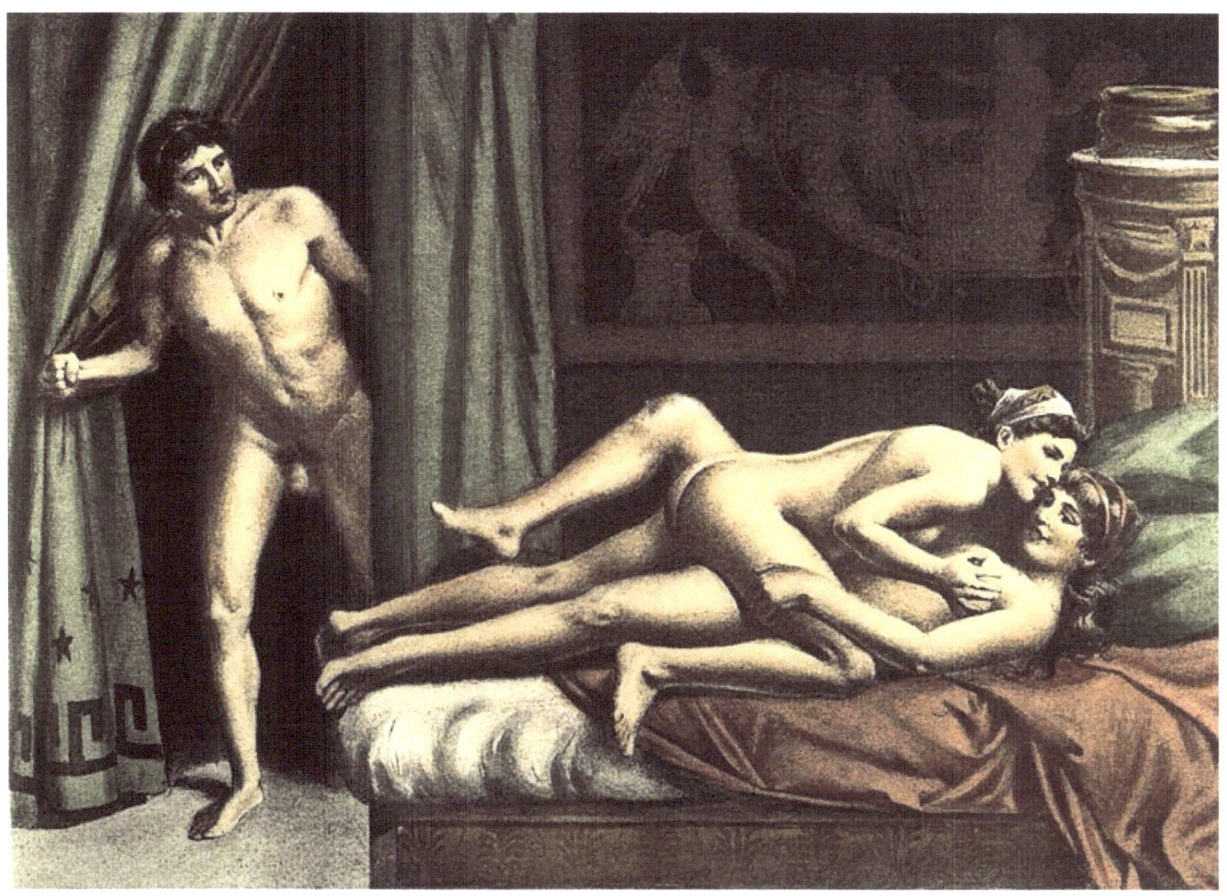

Lesbic sex *De Figuris Veneris*

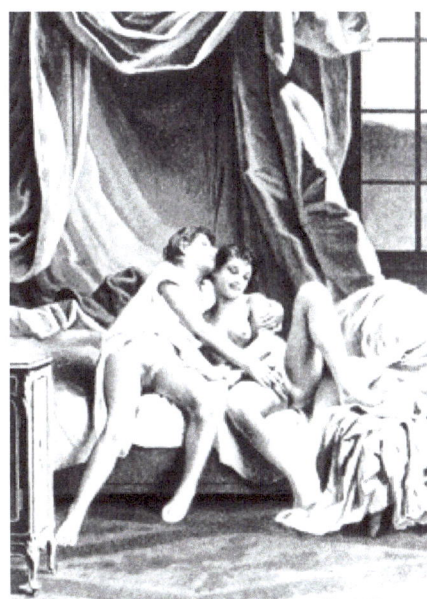

Histoire de Saturnin....., [Charles Hirsch], Paris 1908

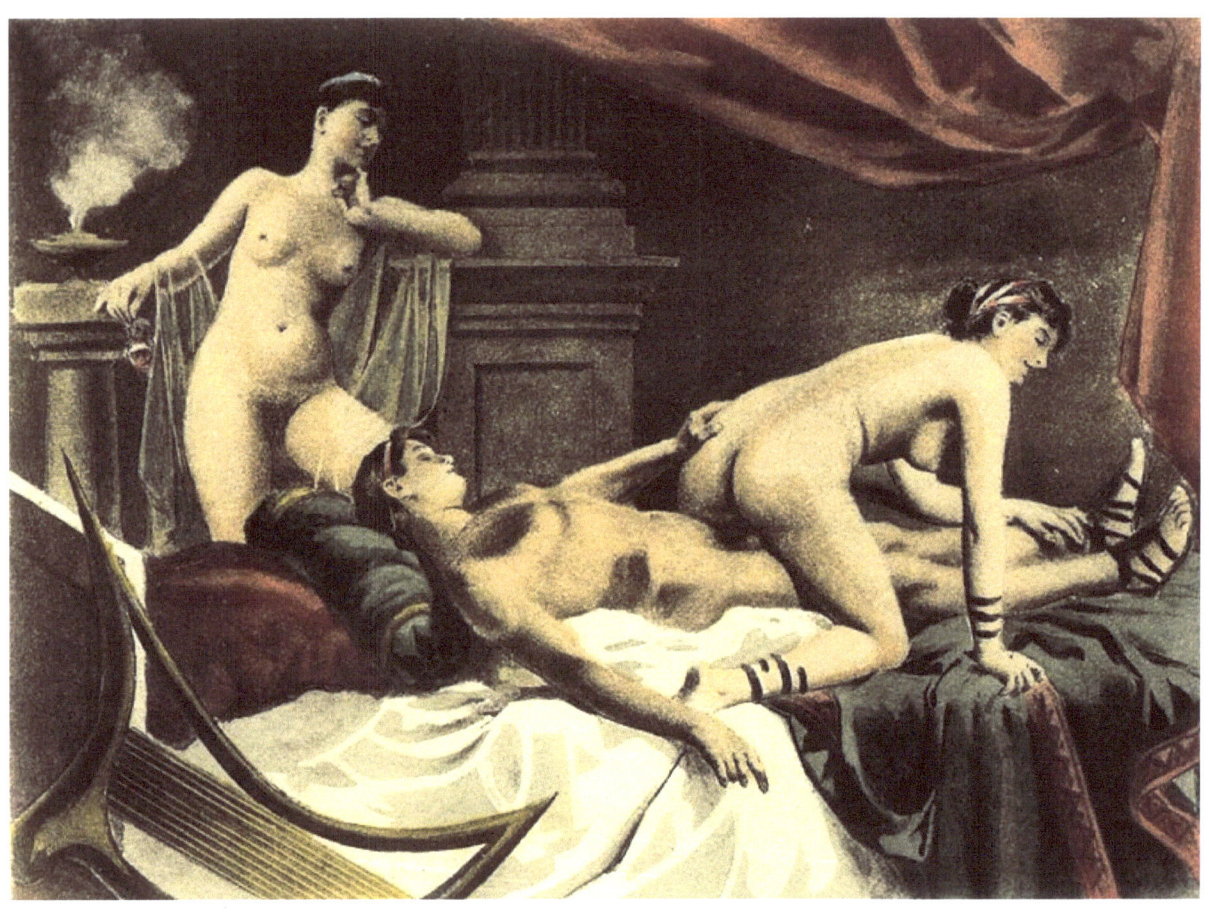

Woman-on-top position--*De Figuris Veneris*